Soul Shaping

DISCIPLINES THAT CONFORM YOU TO THE IMAGE OF CHRIST

Jim L. Wilson

This book was made possible by:
Steve and Barbara Long
2030 Eldorado Lp
Bosque Farms, NM 87068
steve@tendermercychurch.org
Please send them a note of appreciation

Previously published by LifeWay Christian Resources 2009 as the 2010 Doctrinal Study for Southern Baptist Churches.

Dewey decimal classification 248.84

Subject Heading: SPIRITUAL LIFE\DISCIPLESHIP\BAPTISTS-DOCTRINES

www.freshministry.org

www.soulshaping.net

DEDICATION

I dedicate this book to the person who has taught me most of what I know about discipline, spiritual or otherwise—my mother, Barabra Wilson.

ACKNOWLEDGMENTS

This book would not have been possible without those who shared their stories with me so that I could share them with you. I am grateful to each of them for allowing me to tell others about how God is shaping their souls. I also thank them for reading an early draft of their stories to ensure accuracy. To protect their privacy, I have used only their first names or, if they requested, pseudonyms.

I am also thankful to Chris Johnson and David Haney, my LifeWay editors for the first edition of this book. They have both collaborated with me in a collegial way to challenge me to do my best work. While I take full responsibility for any mistakes in this book, I cannot take full credit for all the insights it contains. Thank you, gentlemen. It has been my joy to work with you.

THE AUTHOR

Jim Wilson began preaching at 17 and became a pastor when he was 18. Today, he is the Director of the Doctor of Ministry Program and an Associate Professor of Leadership Formation at Golden Gate Baptist Theological Seminary where he teaches Leadership and Preaching Seminars to DMin Candidates.

Wilson is an award winning writer with hundreds of pieces in print in 60+ publications including some published by Christianity Today, Int., Focus on the Family, and Lifeway Christian Resources.

He is author, contributor or co-author to more than a dozen books, including the Broadman & Holman title, Future Church. His sermons and sermon illustrations appear in Bible Software programs like WordSearch and Logos and he operates www.freshministry.org to provide ministry resources to Church leaders around the world.

Table of Contents

CHAPTER 1: FROM DOING TO LIVING

You've faced them before—decisions. Gut-wrenching, crucial decisions you know will change your life forever. As a Christian, you have spiritual resources you can rely on during those critical times. The problem is, if you haven't prepared yourself spiritually, you won't be ready when those crises come. Your walk with God today will determine what kind of decision you will make when you reach a crossroads in life. Spiritual disciplines are practices you can use in the everyday course of life to maintain a deep, intimate relationship with God. And if your relationship with God is strong, you'll be ready for anything.

DECISION TIME

Darrell stumbled out of bed early so that he could get a cup of coffee at the hospital café before going into her room. He didn't shower or shave but didn't notice. People were moving all around him, but Darrell didn't notice. It was a normal day, but it didn't seem normal. Nothing seemed normal.

Entering the elevator, Darrell turned and noticed something—the first thing he'd noticed all day. The boy was young, much too young to understand why he had lost his hair or why he wore a scar at the base of his skull. The boy looked up from his wheelchair and locked eyes with his father, who placed a reassuring hand on his tiny shoulder—a shoulder much too small to bear the enormity of this pain. The elevator stopped, and father and son walked into the cancer clinic. Darrell turned left into the café and breathed a prayer for the brave boy and his father.

The doctors said it would be a tough day. They were right. Kathryn slept most of the time, drifting in and out. Her goal that day was to sit in a chair three times. Darrell watched as she mustered the strength through tenacity and sheer force of will to accomplish that goal.

Kathryn drifted into sleep as they exchanged good-byes for the night. Darrell drove home in silence, not wanting to hear or think about anything. He just wanted to be home. He wanted life to be normal again. Entering the dark house, he searched for signs of life. There were none—only silence and the echoes of his footsteps in the hall. *You need to rest tonight so that you can be strong tomorrow,* he thought as he crawled into bed. He pulled the covers over his fatigued body and began to cry.

Day 2 was over. There were many more to come.

When Dr. Goff talked to Darrell about the surgery she said, "You've got to take this one day at a time." *Good advice,* Darrell thought. *This is too big to take in all at once.* A few days later the pathology confirmed their worst nightmare. It was stage 3C papillary cirrus, a high-grade cancer. The doctor outlined an aggressive approach of treatment, and the couple consented. The hospital released Kathryn to go home for a week, and soon they would begin phase 2 of the treatment—chemotherapy. On Saturday Darrell did something he knew he shouldn't do: he searched for *primary peritoneal* on the Internet. He was overwhelmed by the results—100 percent terminal!

Chemo isn't a four-letter word, but it should be. Kathryn reacted to the second treatment of chemotherapy. "She became violently ill," Darrell says, "I mean the kind of ill you never want to see a loved one go through— vomiting, diarrhea, difficulty breathing—the works." Is this what life is going to be like? Darrell thought. I don't know if I can do this.

Darrell's life was spinning out of his control. He couldn't control the fact that Kathryn had a terminal form of cancer or that if the disease didn't kill her, it looked like the cure would. He couldn't control his own limitations. He wasn't a nurse, he didn't know how to be a nurse, and he didn't know if he had the strength to be a nurse anyway. In this moment he didn't know whether it would be better to take her back to the hospital. There would be psychological consequences in taking Kathryn to the hospital; it would be taking a step backward. Darrell knew it could crush her morale. What should he do?

This was a defining moment for Darrell. Was this the right time to take Kathryn back to the hospital, or should he wait? The unbelievable turn of events made even the simplest decisions nearly impossible. Yet this wasn't a simple decision. Darrell knew this decision could have life-or-death implications. It wasn't just important that he do the right thing but that he do the right thing at the right time.

Darrell prayed.

TIMING IS EVERYTHING

The period of the judges was the "wild, wild West" of biblical times, featuring battles between Israel and its enemies, the Moabites, the Philistines, the Amalekites, and the Ammonites. One of the judges, Samson, exercised great feats of strength. This colorful character used the jawbone of a donkey as a weapon to defeat the Philistines (see Judg. 15:15) and killed a lion with his bare hands; later he returned and ate honey from its carcass (see Judg. 14:6-9). Another judge, Gideon, was the youngest son from the weakest family in Manasseh; yet God used him to defeat the Midianites and the Amalekites.

Under God's direction he whittled down the army from 22,000 to 300 troops before they attacked and defeated the Midianites with trumpets, fire, and swords (see Judg. 7).

Another judge of Israel was Deborah (see Judg. 4:5). I know I am stating the obvious, but Deborah was a woman. Many people have the mistaken notion that God is sexist. Perhaps they are confusing the Bible's cultural setting with its message. While much of Scripture is set in a repressive culture, the Bible's message is liberating, showing the value of all human life. All people are created in God's image—men and women alike (see Gen. 1:27). Furthermore, all have sinned and fallen short of God's glory (see Rom. 3:23). The apostle Paul gave the definitive word on all humanity's equality before God when he wrote, "There is neither Jew nor Greek, there is neither bond nor

4

free, there is neither male nor female: for ye are all one in Christ Jesus" (Gal. 3:28, KJV).

Deborah was more than just a judge. She was the only judge described as a prophetess.[1] Like Moses before her, she spoke to the people for God during a difficult time in their history. God didn't choose Deborah as a judge and a prophetess to be inclusive. He chose the best person for the job, and she excelled in it.

The times demanded a strong leader. The people of God were captives in Canaan under Jabin, the king of Canaan, and Sisera, his commander. General Barak and his army were doing nothing about the situation, so Deborah summoned him to her court and said to him, "Hasn't the LORD, the God of Israel, commanded [you]: 'Go, deploy [the troops] on Mount Tabor, and take with you 10,000 men from the Naphtalites and Zebulunites?" (see Judg. 4:6).

Deborah took a no-nonsense approach with Barak: she called him out for his laziness, fear, and doubt, demanding that he account for his inaction. She reminded him that God had already promised that He would lure Sisera and his army into a location where Israel's army would prevail against them. Barak agreed to go but only if Deborah would go with him. She consented to go into battle with Barak, but she warned him that his conquest would be void of honor and that he would not defeat Sisera. God would use a woman to do that.

Timing was everything. They needed to launch the attack at just the right time. How would Deborah know when to attack? Ten thousand men followed Barak into battle, while Sisera brought nine hundred iron chariots to the theater of operations. Barak followed Deborah, and Deborah followed God. She depended on Him to know when the time was right.

THE TIME IS NOW!

Something didn't feel quite right to Joyce. She couldn't put her finger on it, but she had a sick feeling in the pit of her stomach telling her to get out of Liberia and to do it now Kenneth and Joyce were already planning to leave the country around July 15, 1990, for a month of well-deserved R & R. They planned to see their family and to spend quality time with Joyce's mother, who was ill. Now for an unknown reason Joyce had a feeling they needed to leave early. Yes, several places in the surrounding area were dangerous, but they didn't give their safety a second thought. The rebels had not advanced on their city; they were 40 or 50 miles away. The danger level had not reached the point that the missionaries in their area felt they needed to evacuate.

Like the climate, the politics in Liberia are hot and humid. In 1980 Master Sergeant Samuel Doe staged a coup, assassinating President William Tolbert and establishing a military government. The Doe regime was brutal, executing 13 officials in public. After some political maneuvering, the country elected Doe president in October 1985. A few years later, officials uncovered a plot to overthrow the government and imprisoned 10 men for 10 years. The next year, in 1989, the rebels began a military offensive to oust Doe from power. The fighting began in the northeast of the country and slithered toward the capital city as the rebel forces took one town after another. By July they had taken the capital city and closed down the airport.[2]

Because of the activity of the rebel forces, Kenneth and Joyce knew they couldn't leave through Monrovia, the nation's capital. They would have to find another way out of the country. So Kenneth took their official papers to a government office to get their exit visas. All his paperwork was in order, but the bureaucrat told him to come back the

6

next day to get his visas. *An inconvenience,* Kenneth thought, *but not a big deal.* He went home and made plans to return the next day. When he returned at the appointed time, the visas still weren't ready; but he opted to stay and wait instead of go home and return later as suggested. The wait paid off; a couple of hours later, he had all the paperwork and began the journey back home.

The next morning the police, the firefighters, the military, and the emigration officials—the very people who had given him their exit visas—had fled the country. Kenneth and Joyce were right behind them, making final preparations to leave. In the capital city Doe's troops turned on civilians, massacring six hundred refugees who had found sanctuary in Saint Peter's Lutheran Church. The danger level had reached the boiling point, and Kenneth and Joyce were just one step in front of the fire. The day they chose to evacuate was the day before the rebel forces entered their city. They were heading for Guinea, a neighboring west-African country 30 miles away. The couple was relieved when they crossed the border, but their relief was short-lived. The river was flooded in front of them; and when they checked on the border crossing back into Liberia, they found that officials had closed it. At the time they didn't know the severity of the threat level in Liberia. Kenneth and Joyce were navigating this trial by instinct. They didn't know their city had been attacked, and they didn't know about the massacre in Saint Peter's Church. All they were working on was the prompting of the Holy Spirit to leave. So what would they do?

This was a defining moment for Kenneth and Joyce. The decisions they would make in the next few minutes would determine whether they lived or died. There was a very real danger behind them, though they didn't know the extent of it. They had to decide whether to go forward, against impossible odds, or turn around and try to get out of the country another day. There wasn't time to gather all the information or to do adequate reflection. With the adrenaline pumping, they needed to make a decision, and they needed to make it now.

One step ahead of falling dominoes, the missionaries decided to go forward; but it wouldn't be easy. The swollen river had washed out the bridge. They had to feel a bit like Moses did as he stood in front of the Red Sea with the sound of approaching thunder from Pharaoh's army closing in on him.

The details are different in each of these stories, but they all have something in common: each person had to depend on God to know what to do and when to do it. God was watching over Darrell, and Darrell was depending on God to know what to do next and when to do it. Deborah had an unusual anointing of God to lead His people. She wasn't depending on her own wisdom or tactical knowledge; she was depending on God and was following His timing. Joyce heard the still, small voice of the Lord to get out of a dangerous country earlier than they had planned. Now at the river they would continue to depend on God for guidance. Significantly, all of these people didn't just need to know what to do; they needed to know God's exact timing—something that is possible only for those who have an intimate relationship with God.

JUST IN THE NICK OF TIME

Darrell and Kathryn's story ended well. Darrell called the doctor and asked for help.

That phone call saved Kathryn's life. They admitted Kathryn to the hospital, and Darrell stayed until almost midnight before going home to get some rest. At one o'clock in the morning, the hospital called. They had moved Kathryn to the ICU because of shortness of breath

8

and a very low heart rate. "There's no reason for you to come in," the nurse said. "We just wanted you to know. She's in good hands." Darrell drifted back to sleep only to be awakened by another call three hours later. "Your wife has thrown two massive blood clots; we need your permission to do a procedure on her. If we do, there is a 10 percent chance that she won't make it," the nurse said.

"What if we do nothing?" Darrell asked.

"If you do nothing, she will die."

Darrell consented, got dressed, and went to the hospital as fast as he could. He didn't know if he'd ever see his wife again. Around ten o'clock the doctor came to the waiting room to give Darrell the verdict: "God must be looking out for Kathryn," the doctor said

"Why do you say that?" Darrell asked.

"If she had not been admitted when she was, you would not have had time to get her here when this happened. She would have died."

Darrell was stunned. "Later that afternoon, after I had time to process this unbelievable event," Darrell says, "I realized its significance. The very thing that caused me to hit the wall—her sickness—was the very thing God used to get us into the hospital on time. It was what saved her life." God's timing is perfect.

GOD'S PERFECT TIMING

When the time was right, Deborah told Barak to attack. Timing was everything.

They needed the element of surprise. Deborah relied on God to give her the wisdom she needed to discern the proper time to give the attack order.

When the army of the Lord descended on Canaan's army, the Lord confused the enemy, and the Lord's army was triumphant. It destroyed everyone except Sisera, who left his chariot and fled on foot to find sanctuary in the home of a friend. The friend's wife welcomed him into their tent and offered him something to drink. Exhausted, he asked her to stand watch for him while he got some sleep. As he drifted off, he didn't know that he would never awake. Using a tent stake, the woman killed him in his sleep. Meanwhile, Barak, filled with confidence from the battle, led a hunt for Sisera. When Barak arrived at the tent, Heber's wife showed Barak Sisera's dead body. As Deborah had prophesied, God used a woman to defeat Sisera. "That day God subdued Jabin king of Canaan before the Israelites. The power of the Israelites continued to increase against Jabin king of Canaan until they destroyed him" (Judg. 4:23-24). God's timing was right.

WHEN TIME STOOD STILL

There wasn't a bridge, but a fallen tree spanned the river. Some locals who were traveling with Kenneth and Joyce put the missionaries' suitcases on their heads and walked across the log. Then it was Kenneth and Joyce's turn. If they slipped, they would fall into a watery grave. The swollen river formed dangerous rapids beneath their feet. With their feet on dry ground on the other side, they counted their blessings. When they discovered the extent of the danger they were in, they thanked God for His watch care over them and for the prayers of His people on their behalf. Joyce says, "All this time we felt at peace. We experienced the peace that passes all understanding. We knew the people at home were praying for us, but we just didn't realize the impact of prayer—that it can give you peace in the midst of chaos."

10

DEFINING MOMENTS

All of these people faced defining moments. Such moments tend to sneak up on people. Rarely do people know they are coming in advance of their arrival. Suddenly, there is an important decision to make. For Darrell, it was when to take his wife back to the hospital. For Deborah, it was when to instruct her general to go into battle. For Kenneth and Joyce, it was when to leave the country. It wasn't as simple as knowing the right thing to do; they all needed to do it at the right time. They all needed the ability to hear God's voice and follow His prompting when their lives were on the line.

This isn't the sort of thing someone can cram for, like a final exam. Being able to recognize God's voice comes from a lifestyle of regularly entering His presence and listening to Him. It's easier said than done. Hindrances like busyness, consumerism, despair, spiritual isolation, and a feeling of entitlement diminish believers' abilities to be in God's presence and experience Him daily. Then when they are faced with their defining moments— moments like Darrell, Deborah, and Joyce faced—they are paralyzed with indecision.

Jesus faced many defining moments. A prime example is His prayer in the garden of Gethsemane (see Matt. 26:36-39). Defining moments never occur in isolation. Behind Jesus' prayer in the garden was a life lived in obedience to the Father, pursuing a single mission of bringing salvation into the world. Jesus didn't live out of fellowship with the Father and then at this defining moment decide to acquiesce to the Father's will. His decision flowed from his life patterns.

In his fatigue and frustration Darrell didn't decide to act in an unselfish manner for the very first time. He had plenty of experience delaying his own gratification for the

11

good of others, whether it was the wife he loved or the congregation he served. This wasn't Deborah's first important decision. She had depended on God to rule as a judge and to speak as His prophetess. Kenneth and Joyce could distinguish God's voice from a premonition because this wasn't the first time they had listened to God. If they hadn't spent a lifetime devoted to prayer and service, they wouldn't have known what to do and wouldn't have escaped danger. All of these people triumphed during their larger-than-life defining moments because of the small things they did every day to cultivate deeper fellowship with God.

WWJD?

In his novel *In His Steps* Charles Sheldon wrote about the members of a mythical Midwestern church whom the pastor challenged to ask the question "What would Jesus do?" before making a decision.[3] As the story develops, those taking Reverend Maxwell's pledge experienced life transformation and sparked a heightened social consciousness in the region. A hundred years later, Christian teenagers wore bracelets with the initials *WWJD* to remind them to ask Reverend Maxwell's question, "What would Jesus do?"

Although I agree that "What would Jesus do?" is a good question, I don't think it is the right question, at least not by itself. Asking what Jesus would do in a given situation without a fundamental understanding of His lifestyle will not give adequate guidance for daily living or for defining moments.

Jesus' lifestyle—His ongoing walk with His Father—shaped His choices. Sheldon's novel seems to reduce Jesus to a model of morality. Jesus is the Savior, not merely a good teacher or a positive role model. It is impossible to understand some of Jesus' words or choices without considering the way He lived His life and the purpose for which He lived.

Everything Jesus did sprang from His redemptive mission. For example, Jesus launched His earthly ministry by turning water into wine. The hosts of a wedding party ran out of wine— a major embarrassment. Mary, Jesus' mother, turned to Him for help. "'What has this concern of yours to do with Me, woman?' Jesus asked. 'My hour has not yet come' " (John 2:3-4).

At first glance Jesus' words do not seem appropriate. Why would Jesus call Mary "woman" instead of "mother"? Was He being disrespectful? He used the same word when He addressed Mary from the cross (see John 19:26), which was actually considered a respectful term[4] when used in direct address. In essence Jesus was saying, "Mother, we see things differently." Mary was concerned with the guests not having wine; Jesus was concerned with His "hour"[5]—the launch of His ministry.[6]

Jesus didn't say these words because He didn't intend to provide wine for the guests; He said them to frame His actions by who He is. Jesus told the servants to fill the six stone pots with water. These weren't ordinary water pots; they contained water for purification ceremonies. When the guests arrived, they used this water source to clean the dirt and road grime off their feet and to cleanse their dirty hands. The water pots were tools of hospitality and good hygiene, but they were much more. They served a religious purpose. A few years later, Pilate, familiar with the custom of the Jews, would wash his hands to proclaim his innocence of the blood of Jesus (see Matt. 27:24). When Jesus turned the Jewish purification water into wine, He was making a bold statement about who He is (the Messiah) and what He came to do (transformation).

Without Jesus' words to his mother, readers could extract a simplistic life lesson from this story: "Do what your mother tells you to do." If they did, they would miss the power behind Jesus' actions. With these words the principle emerges that Kingdom work takes precedence over daily comfort—something Jesus would reiterate in His Sermon on the Mount (see Matt. 6:33) and would demonstrate in the garden of Gethsemane with His prayer "My Father! If it is possible, let this cup pass from Me. Yet not as I will, but as You will" (Matt. 26:39). The way Jesus led His life prepared him for His defining moment in Gethsemane.

Jesus' lifestyle made His choices possible. Dallas Willard writes that the question "What would Jesus do?" falls short because "there is no suggestion that his power to choose rightly was rooted in the kind of overall life he had adopted in order to maintain his inner balance and his connection with the Father."[7] Asking, "What would Jesus do?" without asking, "How did Jesus live?" misses the reasons behind the right choices He made. He didn't just do the right thing; He lived in the right way. One cannot occur without the other.

The believer's goal is not to pretend to be like Jesus when making decisions; it is for decision-making to flow from our core, which God is conforming to the image of Christ. (see 2 Cor. 3:18) It is impossible for Christians to do the right thing during our defining moments if we lose our connection with God during the monotony of life. Or to put it another way, how can you expect to recognize God's voice during crises if you never listen to Him the rest of the time?

Jesus worked, rested, loved, sacrificed, gave, taught, prayed, retreated into solitude, and studied. He didn't just make decisions during defining moments. He lived life in constant contact with the Father, under submission to Him and doing His will. John 5:20 says, "The Father loves the Son and shows Him everything He is doing." The way Jesus lived made His good choices possible.

SPIRITUAL DISCIPLINES

During the late 1970s and early '80s the modern discipleship movement gained traction on college campuses across the country. I remember sitting with other students in a large auditorium filled to capacity and listening to the virtues of one-to-one discipleship. "The most effective way to grow believers is through a 'Paul-Timothy' relationship," the speaker taught. In the foyer he had notebooks for sale that we could use during our quiet times to fill in the blanks until we reached spiritual maturity. We "Timothys" were to submit to our "Pauls" (who had the notebook with the blanks already filled in). After we completed our internships (and had filled in all of our blanks), we found a "Timothy" (who could purchase an additional notebook to fill in) and began discipling him.

Not a bad way to sell notebooks but not necessarily the best way to help a person grow spiritually. The answers to the questions in those books may help a person know about God, but they may not prepare a person to know God. There is a difference. The only way to get to know God is to spend time with Him.

Life is too complicated to fill into anybody's blanks. Spiritual disciplinarians did not help me gain maturity, just guilt. This study takes a different approach. My goal isn't to give you the correct answers to fill-in-the-blanks; rather, it is to nourish your relationship with God and to give you some tools for a lifetime of spiritual growth. Spiritual transformation doesn't take place in workbooks; it takes place in rhythms, structures, and routines.[8] In the 30-plus years that have passed since I shelved my maturity notebook, these are the elements that have helped me grow.

THE RHYTHMS OF LIFE

God uses the rhythms of life—the unforeseen, unplanned, raw moments of each day— to shape me. My most memorable defining moment came after a surgery intended to repair my paralyzed vocal cord. I was facing a lifetime of cashing disability checks but knew I had enough voice to function in society. On a drive across the New Mexico desert, I listened for the heartbeat of God about whether to risk what voice I had left to try another surgery. I had no guarantee that the next surgery wouldn't rob me of what little voice I had. I heard God's voice on that trip: "I called you to preach, Jim. You're in My hands. Trust Me." God healed more than my voice through that step of faith; He worked meekness into my soul. Life happens. God uses the rhythms of life to help us grow.

THE STRUCTURES OF LIFE

God also uses structures—planned events and intentional relationships—to help people grow. These may include worship services, mentoring relationships, and even fill-in-the-blank notebooks. There are two dangers with structures. One is a one-size- fits-all mentality that leads to the spiritual-disciplinarian syndrome. If all you have is a hammer, soon everything starts to look like a nail. For many spiritual disciplinarians, their method is the only way to grow spiritually. The other danger is to toss out all structures because one doesn't fit. The fill-in-the-blank approach to a quiet time didn't work for me, but that doesn't mean other structures haven't benefited me through the years.

16

THE ROUTINES OF LIFE

The chapters ahead focus on some routines that will benefit your spiritual growth within the rhythms of life. The focus isn't on *doing* what Jesus would do but on *living* as Jesus lived. You won't learn a set of rules in this book—no easy, pat answers here. Instead, I want to introduce you to some practices that will help you experience God's presence and grow more like Jesus. These routines, also known as spiritual disciplines, will help you make some subtle shifts in your life:

From consumerism to intimacy

From busyness to focus

From despair to hope

From isolation to connection

From entitlement to ministry

Do you want to have intimacy with God, live a Christ-focused life, have hope, connect with others, and devote your life to serving God? The spiritual disciplines you will encounter in this book can help you move in that direction.

Spiritual disciplines are *small things Christians intentionally do to open themselves to God's work of conforming them to the image of Christ.* You don't have to make major lifestyle changes to practice spiritual disciplines, just some subtle shifts. Don't underestimate the power of small things practiced over a lifetime. John Wooden writes, "There are no big things, only a logical accumulation of little things done at a very high standard of performance."[9] Can small things make a difference?

Spanish bullfighter Jose Maria Manzanares survived 57 bullfights during the 2007 season, including his usual share of goring, trampling, and tossing. The large, powerful bulls he faced never bested him, but the bite of a small mosquito did. Doctors diagnosed the bullfighter with Dengue fever, which he likely contracted by a mosquito bite during a recent tour through Latin America.[10]

As with Manzanares, the greatest dangers aren't always the obvious, big ones. Sometimes the smallest things are the most dangerous. Most campers know the misery of a pinhole leak in an air mattress. Even a small leak can ruin a good night's sleep. No one would take an air mattress on a camping trip with a gash in it. If they saw the hole, they would replace the mattress. The real danger is in the small leaks, not in the big gashes, because the leak is a stealth problem. Small things matter.

Remember this nursery rhyme?

For want of a nail the shoe was lost.
For want of a shoe the horse was lost.
For want of a horse the rider was lost.
For want of a rider the battle was lost.
For want of a battle the kingdom was lost.
And all for the want of a horseshoe nail.[11]

A domino progression begins because of the loss of a small thing, resulting in a catastrophic loss. That ancient rhyme foreshadows why the Titanic sank. In this case it wasn't a misplaced horseshoe nail but a forgotten key. Historical accounts say his superiors reassigned second officer David Blair, the owner of the key, to another ship at the last moment. In his haste to leave the ship, Blair forgot to give the key to Charles Lightoller, his replacement. Because Lightoller didn't have the key, he couldn't open the locker that held the ship's binoculars. Without the binoculars, lookouts in the crow's nest had to rely on their unaided eyesight to scan the horizon for dangers. Because they didn't see the iceberg in time, they couldn't warn the

18

captain of the impending danger. For the want of a key, the Titanic and 1,522 lives were lost. In one sense the iceberg—something very large—sank the Titanic, but in another sense it was a locker key—a very small thing that sealed the fate of the unsinkable ship.[12] Small things matter.

Every time catcher Paul Lo Duca started a game, he scribbled his mother's initials in the dirt behind home plate. Like most children, Lo Duca is sentimental about his mother, who passed away from cancer in 1996; but there is more to the ritual than that. Lo Duca is grateful for what his mom did to help him make it to the show. When he was a youngster, he took batting practice from his mother in their backyard. They didn't use a ball and a bat; instead, she threw pinto beans toward him, and he hit them with a broomstick. Hitting such a small object with such a narrow stick improved Lo Duca's hand-eye coordination and made him a better hitter.[13] Small things matter.

God specializes in using small things to accomplish large purposes.

God used a little boy's sack lunch of two fish and five loaves to feed thousands (see John 6:1-14); five smooth stones and a shepherd boy to defeat a giant (see 1 Sam. 17); and of all the donations he observed in the temple, it was an offering of two mites that Jesus praised (see Mark 12:41-43). Jesus compared the kingdom of God to a mustard seed (see Mark 4:30-32), telling His disciples that even mustard-seed-sized faith can move mountains (see Matt. 17:20). Small things matter.

SPIRITUAL TRANSFORMATION

The purpose behind practicing spiritual disciplines is spiritual transformation, "God's work of changing a believer into the likeness of Jesus by creating a new identity in Christ and by empowering a lifelong relationship of love, trust, and obedience to glorify God."[14] God's goal is for you to become like Jesus—to grow in Christlikeness so that you bring glory to your Heavenly Father. The Bible says, "We all, with unveiled faces, are reflecting the glory of the Lord and are being transformed into the same image from glory to glory; this is from the Lord who is the Spirit" (2 Cor. 3:18).

In Romans 12:1-2, Paul admonishes the reader to be transformed through the renewing of their minds. When hearts and minds align with God's, believers are able to discern His will. Spiritual transformation is not something we can do by our own efforts. It is something God must do. Simply practicing spiritual disciplines doesn't guarantee change. But the disciplines open our hearts and minds for God to speak, convict, and direct. In this way, God can use the spiritual disciplines to teach us, change us, and conform us to the image of His Son. Gary Thomas writes, "Just as failing in one area slowly eats away at our spiritual lives, so improving in one area, even a small one, nourishes our spiritual lives."[15] Great men and women of faith are able to meet the challenges of their defining moments because of the small acts of faith and devotion they build into the rhythm of their lives. In practicing spiritual disciplines, believers are living as Christ lived. As we live as Christ lived, our lives are transformed.

The pages ahead define some key spiritual disciplines and provide instructions for immediately implementing these practices in your life. Over time they will help you recognize God's voice, change your heart, and help you follow His will.

Chapter 2: "From Consumerism to Intimacy"

Arthur Burns was a man of considerable gravity. In the mid-20th century he was the chair of the Federal Reserve, an ambassador to West Germany, and an adviser to presidents from Eisenhower to Reagan. When Burns spoke, Washington listened. Burns began attending an informal White House prayer meeting during the 1970s. Week after week everyone took turns closing the meeting in prayer— everyone, that is, except Burns. Leaders consistently overlooked Burns out of a mixture of respect for his beliefs and reticence. Burns was a Jew.

One week a newcomer led the meeting. Unaware that Burns wasn't a Christian, this person asked Burns to close the meeting in prayer. The old-timers watched Burns, wondering what he would do. Without missing a beat, he reached out, held hands with the others in the circle, and prayed, "Lord, I pray that You would bring Jews to know Jesus Christ. I pray that You would bring Muslims to know Jesus Christ. Finally, Lord, I pray that You would bring Christians to know Jesus Christ."[16]

This chapter will focus on practices that help Christians "know Jesus Christ" — practices like heartfelt prayer, meditation, and celebrating God's presence.

CHAPTER 3: "FROM BUSYNESS TO FOCUS"

Barbara Brown Taylor says, "It does seem to me that at least some of us have made an idol of exhaustion. The only time we know we have done enough is when we are running on empty, and when the ones we love most are the ones we see the least. When we lie down to sleep at night, we offer our full appointment calendars to God in lieu of prayer, believing that God—who is as busy as we are—will surely understand."[17]

Is it possible for well-meaning Christians to become so busy doing God's work that their activities detach them from the God they serve? This chapter will explore how believers can slow down and develop their relationship with God. It will describe some disciplines that help believers maintain focus—unplugging, silence, solitude, and rest.

CHAPTER 4: "FROM DESPAIR TO HOPE"

If anyone should have given up, Sidney Rittenberg could have. The Chinese threw him into jail, where they left him for 16 long years. Within minutes of assessing his dire situation, he recalled a line from Edwin Markham's poem "Outwitted":

> He drew a circle that shut me out,
> Heretic, rebel, a thing to flout.
> But love and I had the wit to win.
> We drew a circle that took them in.[18]

That verse constituted his strategy: he wasn't going to get bitter; he was going to adapt. Warren Bennis and Robert Thomas write, "Evidence of the power of Rittenberg's ability to adapt and survive is Rittenberg Associates, the consulting firm that he founded and continues to run, which helps American companies do business with the Chinese. As his example so vividly reminds us, bitterness is maladaptive."[19] Rittenberg didn't try to get back at his captors on his release; instead, he included them in his circle and built a business model that serves them.

It's easy to let the disappointments of life turn into despair. Instead of giving in to those tendencies, a wise believer practices the disciplines of lament, confession, celebration, and praise.

Chapter 5: "From Isolation to Connection"

Japanese crews preparing a building for demolition found the remains of a man in an apartment and believe the man died alone 20 years earlier. Officials found a skeleton clad in pajamas lying on musty bedding when workers entered the second- floor unit where the man had lived. The date on the newspaper on the kitchen table was February 20, 1984. Authorities say the man worked for a construction firm that built the apartments in 1973. They believe he moved into the vacant building after the firm managing it went bankrupt. They say the man, age 57 at the time, quit coming to work 20 years ago. He was divorced and had children, but none of his family or friends ever asked police to search for him. After hearing the gruesome news, a neighbor said, "I had no idea that the apartment even existed. After I heard the news, I thought, 'Oh, it's here.' It's as if time had stopped in this one place."[20] Although most people don't take isolation to this extreme, some find it easy to drift into isolation and become self-involved and bitter because of life's disappointments. God calls believers to live in community with one another and experience life's full tapestry. People don't need friendly churches; they need friends—people they can count on. This chapter will explore what doing life together looks like and will promote the disciplines of authentic relationships, genuine worship, and true fellowship.

Chapter 6: "From Entitlement to Ministry"

Danielle didn't lose anything; she sacrificed it. She lives an extreme lifestyle as a fulltime missionary to the Jahango people in Africa. For years she considered the call to "take up [your] cross, and follow Me" (Matt. 16:24) as an appeal Jesus gave to special people, not to everyone, until she realized Jesus was speaking to the multitudes, not to the equivalent of God's Special Forces. She came to understand that following Christ meant jeopardizing her life—putting her comfort at risk to follow Christ. "I want to live for the things God values," she says. Though she lives with far less than most Americans, she considers herself rich because she has more than just food and clothing. "Those with more than they need are obligated to jeopardize their excess for the sake of the Lord," Danielle says. "From a global viewpoint and according to the Scriptures, I am rich, because I have more than I need."

Danielle is jeopardizing material things to pursue God and is accepting the consequences of obedience. She isn't just saying, "I love You, God, and will do what You want." She is doing what God wants. This chapter will explore the practices of service and sacrifice.

CHAPTER 2: FROM CONSUMERISM TO INTIMACY

Too often we pray from a position of self-centered consumerism: "God, I need a job." "Please help me get through this project at work." "Lord, please supply the money for my car payment." It's OK to pray about our needs; God cares about them. But He's even more concerned about our hearts. His goal is for us to enjoy an intimate relationship with Him through which He not only supplies our needs but also shapes our hearts to be like His. In this chapter you will practice three disciplines that will help you move from consumerism to intimacy with your Heavenly Father.

A CRY FOR HELP

"Honey, can you come in for a minute?" Rick could tell by the desperation in Karen's voice that she wasn't asking. She needed to see him. "What's wrong?" Rick asked as he wiped the grease from his hands.

"I've been working on the books," she said, "and it isn't good. I made a one- hundred-dollar mistake, and we are going to bounce checks all over town unless we can come up with the money now."

Like most young couples, Rick and Karen had financial challenges. Actually, it was worse than that: they had put everything they had and then some into a down payment for their starter home. They were in debt up to their eyeballs. Karen scrutinized the books down to the last penny. She had to. Their financial survival depended on her ability to stretch every dollar and keep track of every dime. She had made a simple math error, forgetting to carry the 1, and now they were in a bind.

"I don't know what to do either," Rick said, "except to pray." *We tithe every week on our meager income,* Rick thought. *Surely God will be faithful to supply our needs as He promised.* Together they prayed. "God, we need help. We need a miracle. Please provide us with the money we need." When they were done, Rick hugged his bride. "Everything will be OK," Rick said; and he went back to work outside.

As he was changing the spark plugs in the family Volkswagen, Rick noticed a bill on the ground. Immediately, he reached to pick up the dollar, thinking, *One dollar down, $99 to go;* but to his utter amazement there were two zeroes after the 1 on the bill. God had answered their prayer, and he had done it in dramatic fashion just a few minutes after they had prayed.

For Sammy, it didn't materialize that fast; but God provided for his needs too. Sammy heard about a business owner who put a small bookstand filled with Christian literature in his grocery store. *I could do the same thing* Sammy thought, *if only I had a business.* At the time, Anna was working full-time at a hospital; and Sammy was studying in the school of linguistics at Macquarie University in Sydney, Australia, scraping together a living as a part-time janitor at the Sydney Adventist Hospital. With the school expenses and their two kids, they didn't have adequate money to launch a new business. Sammy prayed, "Lord, can You move in Anna's uncle's heart to give us the start-up money for the business?" He said the prayer but then never even told his wife about it. He forgot about it, but God didn't.

While in Indonesia, Anna bumped into an old high-school friend at a market who invited her over to catch up. When she heard about their financial struggles, Lanny asked Anna to follow her into her bedroom. There Lanny opened her safe and took out four gold bars. Before Lanny could say anything, Anna said, "I'm sorry, but I'll be going straight to Sydney and won't have time to exchange the gold for you."

"Don't be silly," Lanny said. "I don't want you to sell the gold for me. I want you to use it to start a business and quit your jobs."

"I could never start a business," Anna said. "It's too risky."

"OK, I'll tell you what," Lanny said. "If you lose it all, then you owe me nothing; but if you make a success of the business, you can pay me back in installments."

God didn't move in Anna's uncle's heart to help them start a business, as Sammy had prayed. Instead, he moved in Lanny's heart. They started a restaurant in

November 1977 and sold it years later to finance their children's college and to start another business in Hong Kong. God answered their prayer, met their immediate need, and paved the way for long-term financial success for their family.

When I was a child, my father was a full-time college student working a part-time job trying to provide for our family of six. Times were tough. Mom became an expert at stretching meals and making something out of nothing. One Sunday night we sat down to dinner; and as was our custom, we gave thanks to God for His provision. But this time it was different. This time there was almost no food on the table. When Dad finished his prayer, we heard a knock at the front door. "I'm sorry to disturb you," the neighbor at the door said, "but I'd prepared this meal for my family's dinner before I knew we had to go out of town tonight. I was wondering if you could use it." That night we enjoyed a feast of southern fried chicken and mashed potatoes. To this day we still enjoy the memory of God's providing us with a plentiful meal after we had given thanks for our sparse rations.

The Bible says, "I have been young and now I am old, yet I have not seen the righteous abandoned or his children begging for bread." (Ps. 37:25). Whether it is a Benjamin on the ground, four gold bars in the safe, or a fried-chicken dinner at the door, God answers the prayers of those who ask for His help.

MORE THAN THINGS

Bill is an addict. Not to drugs or alcohol. Bill's addiction is to jogging. Daily, come rain or shine, he hits the pavement and puts in three to five miles. He was the picture of health—right up until the moment he lay dying on the ground.

28

That afternoon after his run, he started itching all over his body, was lightheaded, and had a growing sense of fatigue and dread. He lay down on the den floor and elevated his feet, trying to force blood to his brain. Instead of lessening his symptoms, this intensified them. He tried to get up but couldn't. He was in trouble—serious trouble. This could be it. *I've fallen, and I can't get up,* Bill thought; but he wasn't laughing. He cried out to God, "Help me make it to the phone." He dragged himself across the floor into the other room to the foot of the desk when he remembered that the buttons on the phone were broken. He had managed to make it across the room but to no avail. *I can't believe it,* he thought. *I'm going to die because I crawled to the wrong phone.* About the time he was going to give up, he sensed God telling him to reach for the phone anyway. He didn't have the strength to grab it, so he walked his fingers up the desk and grasped the phone.

"Lieutenant, I can't get a pulse," the EMT said. Bill wanted to say, "Try the other wrist," but he couldn't muster the strength. They sized up the situation, gave him a shot of epinephrine for anaphylactic shock, and transported him to the hospital.

No one knows for sure what caused the reaction, but today Bill carries an EpiPen® with him everywhere he goes and wears a Medic Alert bracelet with the inscription "Exercise-induced anaphylaxis," and he avoids exercising within three hours of eating smoked meats—the presumed cause of the attack.

When Bill got home from the hospital, he walked over to the desk and picked up the phone that had saved his life. He tried to dial out on it but couldn't. The phone didn't work. It didn't before, and it hasn't since. The only time it worked was the time his life was depending on it—the time God used it to answer his prayer.

With just eight hundred miles on Stephen's new 2003 Limited Corvette, he was itching to try it out to see what it could do. He was heading home on Florida's Chumuckla Highway and floored it. The ponies underneath the hood neighed and started pounding their hooves. The needle on the speedometer raced past the 90 mark to 100 and was headed toward 140 when Stephen lost control around a curve and rolled his ride. With the car upside down and a bit disoriented from the crash, all he could see was the line running down the middle of the road. He struggled to breathe but could take in only a little volume of air at a time.

A passerby notified the authorities, and soon the fire department and paramedics arrived. They jacked up the car and pulled him out. That's when the pain hit him.

Stephen faded in and out until he arrived at the emergency room. The impact had broken all of his ribs, shifted one of his vertebrae downward at a 15-degree angle, broke several other bones, and damaged his shoulder. These injuries were bad but not life threatening. However, blood had filled his lungs. It didn't look as if he would live.

As the word of his condition spread, people across the country started praying for Stephen's recovery. After just three days in the ICU, the pulmonologist removed the endotracheal tube and said, "You're a miracle man. I thought you'd be on the ventilator for at least a month if you lived at all."

Today Stephen is doing fine. God, by His grace, answered the prayers of His people as they asked Him to spare Stephen's life. Stephen believes God spared his life because He still had work for him to do, and Stephen is doing it. Only now he's taking it a little slower around the curves.

JAIL BREAK

Peter was in a world of hurt. He was one of the men imprisoned by King Herod for the sole purpose of persecuting them (see Acts 12:1). Herod was a vicious man. He had already killed James, John's brother. The Jews had approved of that action, so he had captured Peter. Herod had assigned four shifts of four soldiers to the detail, chaining Peter to two of them. Herod's intent was to kill him—but only after giving him a fair trial, of course.

Peter was in a fix. He needed help. He needed a miracle. The church responded by praying. The night before Peter's trial, he slept, chained between two guards. When an angel of the Lord appeared and awoke Peter, he followed the angel's instructions. Half asleep, he put on his robe and sandals and walked out of the prison with the angel past two sets of guards. The angel escorted him to the city gates, which opened by themselves, and Peter walked into the city. That's when the angel disappeared, leaving Peter standing alone—a free man.

Peter went to Mary's house, where people had gathered to pray for him. Rhoda, the servant-girl, could no doubt hear the others praying. When the knock came at the door, she ran to answer it. Who would it be? Was it another member of the church coming to pray? Or was it the Romans coming to break up the prayer meeting and arrest the Christians? No, she recognized his voice. It was Peter. Filled with joy, she failed to let Peter in but instead ran to tell the others that he was there (see Acts 12:12-17).

They didn't believe Rhoda. They said she was crazy. But she insisted. They explained it away by saying it was an angel. But he kept knocking until they opened the door; and sure enough, it was Peter.

GOD ANSWERS PRAYER

God is a God who can! He is the God who walked with the three Hebrew men in the fiery furnace and rescued them from Nebuchadnezzar's evil hands (see Dan. 3:25). He is Daniel's God, who quieted the mouths of the lions and delivered him from their grasp (see Dan. 6). He is Moses' God, who parted the Red Sea and drowned the Egyptian army that pursued God's people (see Ex. 15:4). He is the God of David, who guided the single stone from David's slingshot to Goliath's head (see 1 Sam. 17). He is the God who raised Jesus from the dead and defeated death, hell, and the grave on the first Easter (see Matt. 28:1-8). He is God. He is greater than my understanding or ability to explain. He is the Lord God Almighty.

Jesus said, "Keep asking, and it will be given to you. Keep searching, and you will find. Keep knocking, and the door will be opened to you." (Matt. 7:7). God is ready to answer prayers. He is just waiting for His people to pray.

God answers prayers—even prayers we aren't capable of praying. In his book *When God Interrupts,* M. Craig Barnes writes about a time his pain paralyzed his prayer life. After 36 hours of labor, his wife started hemorrhaging, and the fetal-monitor alarm went off. Doctors and nurses swarmed into the room and asked Craig to leave. He hesitated but knew he had to place his family in the hands of medical professionals. He walked into a cold, abandoned waiting room.

Time stood still, and Craig knew he should pray; but he couldn't. His fear was overwhelming. It appeared that he was about to lose his wife and his child. But even when he couldn't pray, his fear turned to calm. Barnes writes, "My fear of losing my family had become gratitude for receiving it back. When I held my daughter for the first time, that gratitude turned into an overwhelming love. I'll never forget that moment when I met her and fell in love with her at the same time."[21]

Even when we feel that we can't pray or don't know what to pray, the Holy Spirit will pray for us.

CONSUMERISTIC PRAYING

God answers prayers but not to encourage consumerism. Believers don't just pray so that they can get stuff from God; there's more to prayer than that. In I Kings 18 the children of Israel had drifted away from a vital relationship with God. While they had been in the wilderness, their relationship with God had been convenient. They had depended on God for guidance and sustenance. They had been needy, and Yahweh had been their provider. Without the manna He gave, they would have died. But when they reached Canaan, they encountered a new lifestyle and a new god. Baal was the Canaanites' fertility god. The locals taught them that if they worshiped Baal, they would have fertile wives, fertile herds, and fertile crops. The last two, herds and crops, were essential for immediate survival.

The first one, fertile wives, was essential for long-term survival. In the ancient Near East, offspring was essential for financial security during old age. Children honored their father and mother by providing food, clothing, and shelter when their parents were too old to care for themselves.

So what should the children of Israel do? They had to survive, didn't they?

They decided that when in Canaan, they should do as the Canaanites did and worship Baal. It was very practical. After all, they were needy. They had a family to feed and a future to provide for. They worshiped and prayed to Baal for practical reasons, believing he was the god who could meet their material needs. But they couldn't ignore the God of their parents either, so they worshiped and prayed to Yahweh for cultural reasons. Like passing through a cafeteria line, they picked and chose elements from each religion they would follow. Designer faith, if you will. Sounds very 21st century, doesn't it? Does God honor consumeristic prayers?

Does God delight in the consumeristic prayers of needy people—prayers focused on making a person's life easier, better, with more stuff?

Elijah moved in and set up a competition between Yahweh and Baal. Baal's followers would place a sacrifice on an altar and call on Baal to accept the sacrifice and consume it with fire. Elijah would do the same, calling on Yahweh.

The prophets accepted the challenge, and Baal's prophets went first. They gathered a lot of people to pray, prayed for a long time, were exuberant, made a great deal of noise, and even made sadistic sacrifices. Yet their god did not respond, and God's prophet mocked their effort (see 1 Kings 18:22-29).

It doesn't make a difference how many prayer partners are praying, how long people pray, how exuberant their prayers are, how much noise they make, or how much they sacrifice. Prayer to a dead god is ineffective.

Now it was Elijah's turn. Instead of putting dry kindling wood under the sacrifice, Elijah poured gallons of water over it. His prayer did not rhyme. He did not use beautiful metaphors. It wasn't long. Elijah got right to the point. He prayed, "LORD God of Abraham, Isaac, and Israel, today let it be known that You are God in Israel and I am Your servant, and that at Your word I have done all these things. Answer me, LORD! Answer me so that this people will know that You, Yahweh, are God and that You have turned their hearts back" (1 Kings 18:36-37). After this short, humble prayer God responded. "Then Yahweh's fire fell and consumed the burnt offering, the wood, the stones and the dust, and it licked up the water that was in the trench." After God answered, the people worshiped Him, and the false prophets died (1 Kings 18:38-40).

Elijah wanted the people he served to make a choice: they could serve Baal, their health-and-wealth god, or they could serve the one true God. While modern believers would never bow before a fertility god and pray to him, their consumeristic prayers often resemble prayers that Baal's followers would pray. Not that there is anything wrong with children of God asking their Father to supply their needs; actually, there is something very right about turning to God for help. Jesus taught us to pray, "Give us today our daily bread" (Matt. 6:11). But there is a difference between relying on God for needs and approaching prayer as a chance to rub the magic lamp and make three wishes.

DEVELOPING INTIMACY WITH GOD

Prayer isn't just about getting stuff from God. God answers all prayers, but the answer isn't always yes. Sometimes God says no. Three times Paul asked God to take away his thorn in the flesh, but God didn't take it away from him. Why? God had something better for Paul—His grace and power (see 2 Cor. 12:8-9). Paul asked for the healing of his body. God gave him the power of His presence. God's answer helped Paul move from consumerism to intimacy.

Prayer is more than looking for guidance, blessings, or things from God; *it is entering His presence and enjoying an intimate relationship with Him.* When believers have a grocery-list approach to prayer, it can become detrimental to their Christian walk because it makes prayer a means of getting stuff instead of a path to knowing God. It feeds a spirit of consumerism instead of promoting intimacy. The purpose of prayer isn't to get things from God as much as it is to develop a relationship with Him. Don't you think God wants more from prayer than a recitation of needs?

My most intimate relationship is with Susan, my wife. The years have been good to us. Although our marriage hasn't been perfect (how could it be with me as the husband?), it has always been good. While we know we can count on each other for help when we need it, most of the time we anticipate each other's needs and meet them without being asked. But mostly, we pass time together, enjoying each other's company. What if our conversations were just requests for favors? Would we still enjoy the level of intimacy we experience?

Just as spending time with Susan is about deepening our relationship, spending time with God in prayer is about developing intimacy with God. This kind of prayer cannot be prompted by a wish list; it comes from the heart—God's heart. It is leaning into Him, feeling His heartbeat, and dancing to its rhythm. It is entering His presence, not to get something from Him but to be with Him.

For most of my ministry I've taught people to pray by using formulas like the acronym ACTS—adoration, confession, thanksgiving, and supplication—but have failed to teach the deeper truths about prayer. Although those structures teach the basics of prayer, all believers need to get beyond the restrictions of formulas. Why not talk to your Father and listen to Him just because you love Him?

Another date with Ted Koppel, Josephine thinks as she listens to her constant companion, the TV. She carries the hot TV dinner through the hallway into the living room and settles into her Victorian chair for another evening alone. As she peels back the foil, steam rises from her dinner, fogging her glasses. The phone rings. *Who could that be?* she thinks. Josephine takes off her glasses and finds the receiver by the third ring.

"Hello. ...Johnny, so nice to hear from you; it's been so long.... Oh, my, is she all right? ... Of course I will.... Sure.... How much do you need? ... Five hundred dollars? ... That's a lot of money, but I'll find a way.... Nice to talk to you too, Son. Come see me sometime.... Yes, I know you're busy.... I love you."

Where did I put my glasses? Oh, there they are. Her dinner comes into focus. Swiss steak, green peas, and potatoes. Again.

Josephine bows her head and prays. "Thank You, Lord, for Johnny's call. Please help little Jennifer's arm heal. I know how difficult wearing a cast can be for a little girl. And please bless this meal. Amen."

Josephine cuts a small piece of the Swiss steak and turns up the volume on Koppel. *Sure nice to hear from Johnny,* she thinks. *I hope Jennifer will be OK. Sure nice to hear from Johnny. I just wish he'd call when nothing is wrong. Just to talk. Just because he loves me.*

I wonder if God ever feels like Josephine when His children are more anxious to ask Him for things than to spend time with Him.

If you have found yourself devoting more of your prayer time to asking God for stuff than developing an intimate relationship with Him, there are some small changes you can make in your schedule to move from consumerism to intimacy. You can get past the grocery-list approach and the mechanical approach of acrostics and formulas. You can move past consumerism and begin developing intimacy with God through heartfelt prayer, meditation, and celebrating God's presence.

Developing Intimacy with God Through Heartfelt Prayer

Prayer is more than asking God for what we want or need. The discipline of *heartfelt prayer is not a ritual or a list of requests but a relationship you enjoy with your Heavenly Father.* You enter the presence of the Creator to talk with Him and to hear what He wants to say to you.

Heartfelt prayer implies a deep love for our Father and an intense yearning for His presence. The psalmist expressed a longing for God's presence in Psalm 42:1-5

> As a deer longs for streams of water, so I long for You, God. (2) I thirst for God, the living God. When can I come and appear before God? (3) My tears have been my food day and night, while all day long people say to me, "Where is your God?" (4) I remember this as I pour out my heart: how I walked with many, leading the festive procession to the house of God, with joyful and thankful shouts. (5) Why am I so depressed? Why this turmoil within me? Put your hope in God, for I will still praise Him, my Savior and my God.

In such a relationship we find freedom to bring to God our deepest longings, our greatest cares, and our most sincere praise. The psalmist openly confessed his depression and turmoil of soul in verse 5. In God's presence, however, he found hope that led to praise.

Heartfelt prayer runs the range of emotions, from anger to desperation to exuberance. The writers of the

Psalms felt free to express raw emotions that included complaint, accusation, confusion, frustration, disorientation, and more.

Asking God for guidance or help isn't wrong; God wants you to bring your concerns to Him. 1 Peter 5:7 encourages you to cast "all your care upon Him, because He cares about you." Yet prayer is so much more than asking for what you want or need. If your prayers have focused mainly on asking for help, either for yourself or other people, consider how you can also use your prayer time to get in touch with who God is and to continually deepen your relationship with Him.

I'm not suggesting that you stop praying with a list. I'm just encouraging you to examine your list and expand your prayer life to nurture an intimate relationship with your Father.

As with any spiritual discipline, the goal of heartfelt prayer is spiritual transformation. As you deepen your relationship with God, He becomes more real to you, and He teaches you more about Himself and His purpose for your life. Prayer aligns your heart with God's heart so that you learn to know and obey His will each day. Heartfelt prayer prepares you to move into the world to accomplish God's work in His power. Robert Mulholland Jr. writes,

> Prayer is the act by which the people of God become incorporated into the presence and action of God in the world. Prayer becomes a sacrificial offering of ourselves to God, to become agents of God's presence and action in the daily events and situations of our lives. How different this is from the idea of prayer as asking God to change our situation without any involvement on our part![22]

Although meditation is a spiritual discipline that can bring great blessing to a believer's life, it is widely neglected by believers today. Perhaps this neglect is partially due to misunderstandings about the purpose of meditation. Followers of many Eastern religions and New Age cults practice meditation to empty their minds of all thought and to allow what they consider the divine core of their being to come to the surface.

Christian meditation, however, has a very different purpose. Believers should read and study the scripture regularly, but they also need to meditate on Scripture to discover what it says, to reflect on its multifaceted nuances of meaning, to allow the Word to sink in, and then to align our minds and hearts with God's will and purpose, as expressed in that passage. We don't try to empty our minds but to connect personally with God's heart and allow our lives to be filled with the truth of His Word.

Scripture instructs us to meditate on God's Word. Psalm 119 extols the benefits of Scripture meditation.

I will praise You with a sincere heart when I learn Your righteous judgments.

Psalm 119:7

I have treasured Your word in my heart so that I may not sin against You.

PSALM 119:11

I will delight in Your statutes;

I will not forget Your word.

Psalm 119:16

Keep me from the way of deceit, and graciously give me Tour instruction.

PSALM 119:29

Turn my heart to Tour decrees and not to material gain.

Psalm 119:36

How I long for Tour precepts!

Give me life through Tour righteousness.

PSALM 119:40

One way to develop intimacy with God through meditation is to use *lectio divina,* a Latin term that means *divine reading.* When meditating this way, the goal is not to read a large portion of Scripture, pray through a prayer list, or exegete a passage. It is to listen to God—to press into Him.

This type of meditation includes five steps.

First, read the selected text. Let's use Psalm 18:1-2 as an example:

"I love Thee, O LORD, my strength." (2) The LORD is my rock and my fortress and my deliverer, My God, my rock, in whom I take refuge; My shield and the horn of my salvation, my stronghold.

I focus as I read, trying to hear God's still, small voice. I look for words that jump off the page as I read. I circle them. I repeat them. For me the words in these verses that jump off the page are *strength, rock, fortress,* and *deliverer.*

Next I try to visualize the words that impressed me. *Strength* becomes a bulging bicep, a charging bull, or the roar of a full-throttled engine. *Rock* becomes a sheer cliff overlooking Highway 1 along the California coastline. *Fortress* is the locked door that keeps the family safe. *Deliverer* is a big brother defending a child from a bully. I ask myself, *What pictures, smells, sounds, or concepts can I use to experience these words?*

The third step is to begin an honest conversation with God, using the Scripture as my guide. Based on Psalm 18:1-2, I might pray, "Lord, You are my strength, but so many times I rely on my own power to make it through the day. I use my cunning, intellect, wealth, and abilities to manage my own affairs, which usually get me into trouble. Why can't I remember You are my strength? I need Your strength right now to be able to minister today. The people I will see have problems I can't fix. Be my strength, O Lord.''

Then I repeat these words and allow God to whisper encouragement into my heart.

In my sincere prayer I hear God say, "I am your strength, Jim. In your weakness I am made strong. I will glorify Myself through you today as you rest in Me." Throughout the day I listen to see how God speaks to me through the passage.

As my day ends, I consider how God spoke to me throughout the day. I think about the couple I met with whose marriage was falling apart and how I was able to say with conviction, "God will be your strength in this trial. Depend on Him." I think about my children's challenges and how I can be assured that God will provide for their needs. Though this process I experience God.

Now it's your turn. Practice meditation by focusing on Psalm 94:17-19.

Focus as you read the verses. Read them multiple times, emphasizing a different word each time. What words jump off the page as you read?

Circle them. Repeat them.

Now visualize those words. What pictures, smells, memories, or phrases can you use to experience these words?

Have an honest, free-flowing conversation with God, prompted by the Scripture.

As you continue to reflect on the words you've highlighted, listen to God's encouraging voice as He whispers back to you. Listen for Him to speak through the passage throughout the day.

At the end of the day, consider how God has encouraged you throughout the day, using the verses you've selected.

Developing Intimacy with God by Celebrating His Presence

A third way to develop intimacy with God is to practice His presence. This is the discipline of breathing a prayer of adoration when you see a sunset or a prayer of praise as you hold a loved one's hand. Sometimes it is pausing to celebrate God's goodness in the middle of the day. Other times it is looking beyond the disappointment of a prayer He is saying no to and beholding His glory.

One of the most reassuring truths we can hold on to in good times and bad is the God's constant presence (see Psalm 139). Because we live in His presence, we can call on Him, praise Him, or just talk to Him at any time of the day or night.

We can't escape His presence even if we try. God even knew us before we were born, for He is the One who made us. Be overwhelmed by both God's omniscience and His omnipresence, and then respond with praise and celebration.

Mother's Day isn't the easiest day for Cheryl to go to church. It isn't that she resents the pastor's giving roses to mothers or recognizing the oldest and youngest mothers and the one with the most children. She just wishes that sometime during the service someone would recognize the women who long to be mothers but can't.

Mother's Day is tough, but there's also the monthly reminder that she isn't pregnant and the occasional insensitive question "So when are you and Bill going to start a family?" For the first seven years of their marriage, that was an easy question to answer. They had decided not to have children, but then they changed their minds and wanted to get pregnant but couldn't. Cheryl's doctors tell her there is no physical reason she can't have a child. In a way, that makes it worse. Every month she waits, and every month the emotional distress accompanies the physical discomfort. Yet in another way it makes it easier, because she knows this is in God's hands. She will get pregnant if He wants her to.

But why wouldn't He want her to? Why doesn't God wish to bless Cheryl with children? Is it punishment for not wanting children at the beginning of their marriage? She watches as the other women in the church get their roses on Mother's Day. It isn't the roses. She can buy her own roses. It's what they symbolize—the blessings of God in these families. Why won't God bless her? It isn't the recognition she craves; it's the blessing. Why does God bless all these women with children but not her?

Sometimes Cheryl longs for God's blessings; other times she doesn't even expect God to bless her. Maybe that springs from the garden variety of insecurity that everyone experiences, or maybe it's a childhood flashback. Cheryl's dad was better at drinking his paycheck than using it to provide for his family. Early on, Cheryl learned not to

44

expect what her friends had—not just things like toys, clothes, or food but also things like peace when she got home from school. It was tough when her dad wasn't there, especially on her mom, who had seven kids to look after; but it wasn't a cakewalk when he was home either. When he was there, Cheryl helped her mom corral the other kids and keep them quiet and out of her dad's hair. Anger, resentment, and want, not peace, filled her home.

Cheryl wanted to provide a home for her unborn children that she never had. Why won't God let her? Why did she have the kind of home she grew up in, and why won't God give her a chance to build a godly home for someone else? With time she's been able to release the bitterness over her childhood, forgiving her parents and asking God to shower His grace on them. But letting go of the current pain is harder. Other women who have gone through similar circumstances have wished for death.

Rachel's struggle with infertility was miserable. The Bible says, "When Rachel saw that she was not bearing Jacob any children, she envied her sister. 'Give me sons, or I will die!' she said to Jacob" (Gen. 30:1).

Jacob had worked seven years to win Rachel's love. I don't mean he courted her for seven years; I mean for seven years he did work for her father in exchange for the right to marry Rachel. After what seemed a lifetime of waiting, the big day arrived; but it didn't turn out as he expected. For Jacob, there was mourning in the morning: he discovered Leah, not Rachel in his bed. His father-in-law had tricked him and pawned off Leah on Jacob. Jacob wasn't happy. The Bible gives us a clue why. Rachel was beautiful; Leah wasn't (see Gen. 29:17). Jacob agreed to work for another seven years for Rachel's hand, but this time he got his payment up front. However, all was not well in paradise. Not only did Rachel have to share her husband with her sister, but also Leah was giving Jacob children, while she wasn't. Rachel was so sad that she was ready to die.

Hannah reacted to barrenness in a similar way. The Bible says, "Deeply hurt, Hannah prayed to the LORD and wept with many tears." (1 Sam. 1:10). This was a woman with a heavy heart. One reason for her pain was that her husband's other wife teased her, without mercy, because Hannah was barren. *Barren*—a harsh word for a harsh reality in her culture. In many ways her worth, her justification for existence hinged on her having children; or at least she thought so.

Hannah was persistent in her prayer. 1 Samuel 1:12 says, "She continued praying before the LORD," and in verse 15 she said, "I am a woman oppressed in spirit." The word *oppressed* has a stubborn, determined connotation. A strong desire drove her; she was persistent as she prayed. She rushed the throne of grace to make her request. She came ready to state her case before God, and state it she did —not in an arrogant, demanding way but in humility.

When Hannah poured out her soul in prayer, she made a vow to the Lord:

"LORD of Hosts, if You will take notice of Your servant's affliction, remember and not forget me, and give Your servant a son, I will give him to the LORD all the days of his life, and his hair will never be cut." (1 Sam. 1:11). She wasn't bargaining with God. She promised to give her son back to God. She wasn't praying her will. She was praying God's will, evidenced by the fact that she wasn't praying for a son to have but a son to give—a son who would be a champion for God and would walk in His will, a son committed to God from the womb to the grave. And God gave her what she requested: "After some time, Hannah conceived and gave birth to a son. She named him

46

Samuel, because [she said], "I requested him from the LORD." (1 Sam. 1:20).

God gave Hannah the desire of her heart. God also opened Rachel's womb, and she gave birth to two sons. Why did God make these women wait? In Hannah's case it was so that she would dedicate Samuel to the Lord's work; in Rachel's case it was to help her grow. Rachel had probably spent her whole life thinking she was better than Leah. I suspect her struggle with infertility sanded some rough edges off her soul. These hardships would lead either to bitterness or to peace. For both of these women, they led to peace.

But why doesn't God bless Cheryl with children as He did Rachel and Hannah? Sometimes God answers people's prayers yes, giving them the desires of their hearts. Other times He answers their prayers no, at least not now, while using their disappointments to heal their wounds, set them free, and mold them into His image.

Cheryl is finding peace in her pain. God spoke to her while she was reading *The Purpose- Driven Life* by Rick Warren. She sensed Him asking her to wipe away her tears and to consider how her relationship with Him was going. When she read about the importance of being candid with God and that bitterness is the greatest barrier to friendship with God, she had to admit her own bitterness. Her defiant heart whispered to her, *Yeah, well, God caused the pain. When He cures it, then we can talk, about honesty.* But her defiant heart didn't win out. When Cheryl read a C. S. Lewis quotation stating that pain is God's megaphone, she realized God was trying to speak to her in her pain. She was saying to Him, "Take away the source of my pain," while He was saying to her, "Drop your defiance, and I'll speak to you through the pain." That day Cheryl prayed, "Father, I long for my praise and worship to be fragrant to

You. More importantly, I long to be important to You. I long for meaning and significance. I want to be special. I don't understand why normalcy has never been possible for me—why I can't be a mother."

God hasn't blessed Cheryl with children, but He has blessed her with the ability to celebrate His presence. Although this relationship will never squelch her longing for children, a houseful of children could never replace the connection she now enjoys with God. Cheryl hasn't gotten what she wanted, but she has gotten what she needed— intimacy with God. Often it is in the darkest moments of life when we experience God most clearly.

Practicing the presence of God is not limited to praising Him while reflecting on His attributes or reflecting on life through theological lenses. It also involves recognizing the touch of His unseen hand.

"You need to just go home and get on with your life," the doctor said. "Your husband is not going to recover." Barbara was devastated. She couldn't believe it would end this way. Barbara and Jimmy had been married in September 1945, the same month World War II ended. Jimmy hadn't come back from the war in one piece; he had lost a leg and had taken on some shrapnel the doctors were unable to remove. But now he had slipped into a catatonic state. He wasn't unconscious, but he wasn't all there either. He was sent to Denver, where he could get the treatment he needed. Barbara had already farmed out the kids to relatives so that she could go with him, hoping against hope they could help him. Now they had ruled out a tumor, but they didn't know what the problem was. All they knew was that the probability for recovery was slight and that Barbara would be better off if she moved on. Her mother-in-law agreed. "Go ahead and divorce Jimmy, and I'll bring him home with me," she said.

Barbara couldn't do it, partly because 15 years before, she had stood before God and His witnesses and had promised to stay married to Jimmy in sickness and in health. But it was more than that. It was more than doing the right thing. Barbara trusted God. She hoped He would make things right. As she weighed her options, she remembered the way God had comforted her during Jimmy's first day at the hospital.

As Barbara was walking out of the VA hospital in Albuquerque, she had thought, *The rest of my life is going to be different.* When Barbara told her mother-in-law about it, she said, "Oh, you're just being pessimistic. Everything is going to be fine." That night Barbara lay in her empty bed in her empty house and cried out to her Father from her empty soul. A passage of Scripture from Isaiah came to her mind: "Fear thou not; for I am with thee: be not dismayed; for I am thy God: I will strengthen thee; yea, I will help thee; yea, I will uphold thee with the right hand of my righteousness" (Isa. 41:10, KJV). Instinctively, Barbara lifted her right hand, with her elbow against the mattress, and drifted off to sleep. "He held my hand all night," Barbara says. "I could feel the warmth of His hand in mine."

Barbara didn't know the future; she just knew her life would never be the same and God would be with her. For more than a year Jimmy stayed in Denver, and Barbara held God's hand. The remainder of Barbara's life was different, just as she thought the first day Jimmy was in the hospital. God gave her the serenity to accept what she couldn't change. She couldn't change Jimmy's situation, and God gave her the peace she needed to get through the trial. He also gave her the courage to do what she could: she remained faithful to her husband and trusted in God. He didn't fail her. She was never alone. And neither was Jimmy.

Jimmy's awakening came during a chapel service at the VA hospital in Denver as the patients sang "Never Alone." This hymn, based on the promise of Scripture that says, "I will never leave thee, nor forsake thee" (Heb. 13:5, KJV), had streamed through Jimmy's mind while he was still in darkness. Now he was singing it, in the light, with everyone else.

> No, never alone,
> No, never alone,
> He promised never to leave me,
> He'll claim me for His own.
> No, never alone,
> No never alone.
> He promised never to leave me,
> Never to leave me alone.

On their 50th wedding anniversary I watched Jimmy and Barbara hold hands and renew their wedding vows. I got a little choked up as I listened to them say the words "in sickness and in health." They weren't just words to them; they were a lifestyle. A lifestyle of intimacy. Intimacy with one another, yes; but there was another intimate relationship there. There was an unseen hand in the auditorium that day—the hand of a God that held Barbara's through the night and that guided Jimmy through the darkness.

Even in the midst of darkness, Barbara celebrated God's presence; and even though Jimmy was unconscious, he did too. As God had promised (see Psalms 23:4), He was with them.

The reason believers sometimes feel alone during their difficult days isn't that God has forsaken them; it's because they have failed to recognize His presence. Jimmy practiced God's presence, even in the darkness, as the words of "Never Alone" wafted through his unconscious mind. Barbara celebrated God's presence by holding on to His unseen hand in the darkness. God's presence surrounded both of them, and they celebrated it.

One practice that helps you celebrate God's presence is to take a few minutes every day to write down ways you observe God working in your daily life. Take a moment to reflect on God's unseen hand in your life.

What is happening now that gives you concern?

Is there anything you are honestly grateful for? If so, what is it?

What feelings are you are experiencing as you reflect on life?

What is making you sad, angry, glad, disoriented, or worried?

Can you see or imagine God at work in your circumstances?

How is He drawing you to Himself?

What is God teaching you? Is there a chance you are asking for something good, and He is giving you something better?

What does He want you to hear from His heart to yours?

After writing, pray about what you have written. Express to God your fears and concerns, as well as your desire to know Him intimately and to let Him conform your heart to His.

You've just completed your first journal entry. Now write another entry each day for the next month. Record your heartfelt prayers and make notes as God speaks to you. This practice will help you learn to celebrate God's presence every day and to know Him better through prayer.

Don't cheat yourself out of knowing God because the only time you talk to Him is to ask Him for stuff. Beyond praying for items on your prayer list, pray heartfelt prayers that focus on your relationship with your Father. Take time to meditate on His Word and to celebrate His presence. God will use these disciplines to conform you to Christ's image.

CHAPTER 3: FROM BUSYNESS TO FOCUS

Perhaps the most pervasive complaint in our fast-paced, high-stress world is that we are all too busy. Sometimes it seems that our lives are a whirlwind of activity without any direction or purpose. Even Christians can get so busy that we don't have time to minister to other people or, even worse, to spend time with God. If we are too busy for God, does anything else really matter? This chapter will give you some tools for restoring focus to your life. Practicing the following disciplines will help you live with single-minded devotion to God and orient all of your activities around your relationship with Him.

MISSING IN ACTION

As the pastor of two rural churches in Colorado, Dan stays busy. Like most pastors, he has plenty to do; but he has twice the committee meetings and twice the worship services.

When Dan's daughter was in the third grade, her teacher requested a parent- teacher conference with him. His wife usually took care of those conferences; but the teacher insisted on seeing him, not his wife. When she wouldn't take no for an answer, Dan made the appointment to drop by the school in the afternoon. "I wanted you to see this drawing your daughter made of your family," the teacher said.

Dan looked at the picture and asked, "Where am I?"

"That's why I called you down here today," the teacher responded. "I asked your daughter the same question. She said you're never home, so she left you out of the picture."

Dan had been busy doing the Lord's work. It was noble work. People benefited from his hard work and dedication, but his family was suffering.

THE STRUGGLE FOR BALANCE

In Harry Chapin's song "Cat's in the Cradle"[23] a father struggles to find time to spend with his son because of the demands of work and life. The boy asks for his father's attention, the father says "later," and the boy responds each time by saying he wants to grow up to be just like his dad. By the end of the song, the boy is grown, the father's life has slowed down, and he is ready to make up for lost time; but the son doesn't have time for the father. He is busy with other demands and can't seem to fit his father in. Chapin

54

delivers the knockout punch when the father acknowledges that his son had grown up to be just like him—a man who is too busy to spend time with his family.

I hate that song.

I've lived on both sides of that scenario. I know what it's like to be a son, longing for the attention of my busy father, and I know what it's like to look in the disappointed eyes of my own boys as I walk out the door to fulfill my obligations.

The guilt I'm feeling right now isn't fair. One way I loved my boys was to earn a living. When they were young, someone had to pay for their diapers; and when they were older, someone had to make their tuition payments. Andy Stanley writes, "There is nothing honoring to God about the workaholic who neglects his or her family. But the man or woman who refuses to provide for his family brings no honor to Him either."[24] Somewhere there is a balance.

Beyond the normal struggle to find a balance between home and work obligations, the work I was doing was noble work. I wasn't just working a job; I was fulfilling a calling—a calling from God to go where He sent me and to do His work. Too many times our family outings were interrupted by a phone call from someone needing care, but I couldn't sit at the baseball stadium with my family eating a hot dog while someone was dying in a hospital across town. The hard reality is that there are times when a family has to understand.

TOO BUSY FOR GOD

My family isn't the only relationship I've neglected to do the Lord's work. I've also neglected my relationship with the Lord. Over the years there have been periods when the only time I studied the Bible was to prepare a sermon and when my prayers were not so much an intimate conversation with God as an occasion to tell God what I thought He should do. In short, there have been seasons in my life when I was too busy serving God to spend any quality time with Him.

I'm not alone. The Obstacles to Growth Survey polled 20,000 believers from the ages of 15 to 88 across 139 countries. On average, in North America, 62 percent of Christian women and 61 percent of Christian men say busyness gets in the way of developing their relationship with God.[25]

Michael Zigarelli, an associate professor of management, says, "The accelerated pace and activity level of the modern day distracts us from God and separates us from the abundant joyful, victorious life He desires for us." He describes the problem as "a vicious cycle" driven by cultural conformity. Zigarelli says busyness may be a global pandemic. He suggests that Christians break the cycle by "reordering our thinking," including "the way we think about who God is and how he wants us to live our lives."[26] It appears that Christians have come to believe that busyness is virtuous. Bruce Demarest writes,

> The Bible affirms the virtues of "faith, hope and love" (1Corinthians 13:13) and to that many Christians add a fourth virtue: busyness for God. Many find that the crush of daily life prevents them from really relating even to their spouse or children. Communion with the God of the universe? Who has time for that? And then from the pulpit were challenged to roll up our sleeves and get busy for God. The pastor of the church in which I was raised urged us to

56

"burn out for Jesus!" as if a total breakdown makes you a good Christian![27]

Everybody gets busy. The problem isn't getting busy but staying busy, needing to be busy, and choosing busyness as a lifestyle. Instead of staying busy living out their purpose, some people seem to make busyness their purpose for living.

THE PROBLEM WITH WORKS

From the beginning of my Christian walk, Ephesians 2:8-9 occupied a special place in my heart. I suspect I am not alone. Many Christians can quote the verses. But most Christians stop quoting too soon. Verses 8-9 explain the means of salvation, while verse 10 explains the reason for salvation.

Ephesians 2:8-9 explains that we are saved by God's grace. Ephesians 2:10 gives the reason for salvation—so that we can walk in the good works God prepared for us. Paul wrote these words. Paul experienced these words. One afternoon he was traveling to Damascus to round up any people belonging to the Way and bring them back to Jerusalem, where they would receive a fair trial before their execution. On the road he didn't meet anyone belonging to the Way, but he did meet the Way, the Truth, and the Life (see John 14:6). Saul, as Paul was known then, met the resurrected Lord. A bright light—the bright and morning star—blinded him, and Saul dropped to the ground. Disoriented, he followed the voice's instructions, went into the city, and waited.

While Saul was following God's instructions, God was also giving instructions to Ananias. He was to go and meet Saul at Judas's house and minister to him. Ananias wasn't convinced he wanted to follow God's instructions. After all, he knew this man's reputation and his authority to arrest believers (see Acts 9:1-14). God said, "Go! For this man is My chosen instrument to carry My name before Gentiles, kings and the sons of Israel" (Acts 9:15). The reason God gave for choosing Paul was that He had work for him to do. God saved him so that he could serve. God saved you for good works too. Ephesians 2:10 is clear about that.

The problem comes when our works turn into a lifestyle of busyness. After delivering a lecture on the spiritual life of a leader in a class at Golden Gate Baptist Theological Seminary, I gave the students the assignment to select something they could stop doing that was a waste of time and to replace it with a spiritual discipline.

How would you complete that exercise? What could you stop doing that is a waste of time to make room in your schedule to practice a new spiritual discipline?

One of my favorite responses was from a student who planned to start recording sporting events on his DVR instead of watching them live. He planned to fast-forward through the commercials during playback and use the time he saved to meditate on Scripture.

Not a bad exchange. This student would invest his time meditating on Scripture instead of wasting time watching commercials. Another student wasn't so quick to participate.

He wanted to know what was wrong with being busy. "Isn't that the goal?" he wrote, I didn't dismiss his question. I understood what he meant. He was referring to a healthy state of being occupied doing what God created him to do—to be faithful regardless of the personal sacrifice—like Peter and John's reaction to their rebuke by the Sanhedrin (see Acts 4:19-20). This student understood sacrifice for the sake of the gospel. He commuted over three hours to be in the class that day and would drive back home when it was over. On staff at a leading churches, he was busy doing God's work. We were using the same word, *busy,* but in different ways. He meant occupying himself with what God had called him to do; *I meant a relationship-destroying, constant stream of endless activity.* I wrote back to him, "No, the goal isn't to be busy; it is to be faithful." Sacrifice is a spiritual discipline (see chap. 6)—a small thing Christians intentionally do to open themselves to God's work of conforming us to the image of Christ—but it should lead a believer closer to God, not farther away. When sacrifice gets toxic, it starts harming, not helping, a Christian's relationship with God.

God didn't save us solely to work for His kingdom; He also wanted us to be in relationship with Him—to walk in His sight, holy and blameless. Paul wrote, "He chose us in Him, before the foundation of the world, to be holy and blameless in His sight. In love He predestined us to be adopted through Jesus Christ for Himself" (Eph. 1:4). Busyness becomes a problem when it harms a believer's relationship with God. Henry and Richard Blackaby write:

> God uses our activities and circumstances to bring us to Himself. When He gives us a God-sized assignment, its sheer impossibility brings us back to Him for His enabling. When God allows us to go through crises, it brings us closer to Him. If we are not careful, we can inadvertently bypass the relationship in order to get on with the activity. When you are busy in your activity for God, remember that God leads you to the experiences in order to bring you to Himself.[28]

Busyness can become a downward spiral of doing God's work but not doing the work God created each believer to do. Jesus told the parable of the Good Samaritan to portray good works that God honors (see Luke 10:25-37). When Jesus told this story, His Jewish listeners had probably never heard the two words *good* and *Samaritan* together. Jews despised Samaritans. Extrabiblical material calls them "the foolish people who dwell in Shechem." Shechem is referred to elsewhere as a "city of fools."[29] The New Testament reflects a clear divide between Jews and Samaritans (see John 4:9). It would not have surprised Jesus' audience if the priest or the Levite had rendered aid without regard for reward. That is what religious people are supposed to do. But to Jesus' listeners, it was outlandish that the Samaritan did. And that is the point of this parable: a man these Jewish listeners despised was the one with real virtue. Not the priest. Not the Levite.

A despised, despicable Samaritan was the neighbor.

What makes this parable great isn't that a stranger rendered aid to a crime victim and provided long-term care for him. It's that the stranger who did it was a Samaritan. Jesus didn't define *neighbor* as someone who shares your morals, interests, economic status, and religious beliefs. He didn't say neighbors are people you feel comfortable being around. A neighbor, in this parable, is a despised person who acts like a neighbor.

Although it is right to focus on the action of this despised man—he is a timeless example of living the second demand of the Great Commandment, "Love your neighbor as yourself" (Mark 12:31)—it is also helpful to notice the actions of those who didn't render aid to the hurt man. Why didn't they stop and help? Perhaps you've heard preachers explain that the priest and the Levite were probably too busy doing God's work to help. But that doesn't make sense—especially in light of the Great Commandment, which lists loving God and loving neighbors as life's greatest priorities. Is it possible to have the right priorities but fail to practice neighborly love because of life's demands?

In *Tipping Point* Malcolm Gladwell describes an experiment John Darley and Daniel Baston, two Princeton University psychologists, conducted with theology students, based on the parable of the Good Samaritan. Darley and Baston gave the students a questionnaire to find out why they were studying theology. Then they asked the students to prepare a speech on one of two subjects. One group would talk about the relevance of the professional clergy, and the other group would speak on the parable of the Good Samaritan. Next, the students were instructed to walk across campus to deliver their talks. Before the experiment's administrators dismissed the students to deliver their talks, they told them something to the effect of "You're late; you'd better get going" or "It will be a few minutes, but you may as well get started now."

The psychologists didn't tell the students they would not evaluate them on their speeches but on what they did on the way to deliver them. Darley and Baston had arranged for an actor to be on the path, playing the role of the wounded man in the parable. Some of the harried ministers going to deliver the speech on the parable of the Good Samaritan did not "pass by on the other side." They literally stepped over the hurting man! Malcolm Gladwell writes, "The only thing that really mattered was whether the student was in a rush. Of the group that was, 10 percent stopped to help. Of the group who knew they had a few minutes to spare, 63 percent stopped."[30] Can you believe it? Theology students who just prepared sermons on the parable of the Good Samaritan were too busy to stop and help a suffering person. Busyness kept them from fulfilling their calling. Gary Thomas writes, "Any number of deeply felt crises are going on in people's lives, but in our busyness, our lack of expectancy, we miss opportunities to minister to people in supernatural ways."[31]

MAINTAINING FOCUS

Why would believers become so busy doing God's work that they risk alienating their families, weaken their relationships with God, and lose opportunities to minister in Jesus' name?

One cause of busyness—*a constant stream of endless activity*—occurs when Christians try to earn their worth through accomplishments. Bruce Demarest writes,

> Why do we drive ourselves so relentlessly? We schedule ourselves to the eyebrows to make the best impression or to prove our worth. We distort the philosopher Descartes' maxim 'I think, therefore I am,' to read, 'I work hard, therefore I am.' Some relish busyness and speed to avoid facing up to their real selves and the haunting emptiness within.[32]

Solomon discovered the emptiness of using accomplishments as a substitute for intrinsic worth. Before his bout with workaholism, he lived the "good life," spending all of his time and energy searching for the ultimate good time. His search for pleasure left him empty; so he turned to the bottle, trying to find relief from his disappointment. Failing to get relief, he judged his time in the bottle as a foolish way to live. After Solomon turned from wine, he threw himself into his work. He built huge homes and gardens and worked hard at being king. His kingdom increased and became greater than that of any other king before him.

Solomon didn't find his true sense of worth in pleasure, wine, or hard work. He found it only through his relationship with God. He wrote, "There is nothing better for man than to eat, drink, and to enjoy his work. I have seen that even this is from God's hand. For who can eat and who can enjoy life apart from Him?" (Eccl. 2:24-25) In the context of a vibrant relationship with God, pleasure and work both have their place; but when pleasure or work becomes a substitute for that relationship, it becomes toxic.

After a lifestyle of distraction, Solomon finally learned to focus his life on what mattered most. In Ecclesiastes 12:13-14 he wrote, "When all has been heard, the conclusion of the matter is: fear God and keep His commands, because this is for all humanity. For God will bring every act to judgment, including every hidden thing, whether good or evil."

Like Solomon, believers today are also given to the same soul sickness of busyness. Solomon chased meaning through armies, wealth, and fleshly pleasures. Too often believers are sidetracked by the priorities of the world, like career, materialism, and entertainment.

In addition, we often chase meaning through religious activities involving committees, programs, and church meetings. These things can be good if God has called us to do them. If not, they are distractions from the real assignments He has for us; and they may feed our need to bolster our self-esteem, to control, or to be involved in constant activity. James 4:7-8 warns us not to be "double-minded people" but to draw near to God—to orient our lives around Him. Solomon abandoned the need for world-conquering activities to find rest and meaning with God.

We should examine all of our activities to make sure they are leading us to give priority to God's work in us.

Robert Mulholland Jr. writes, "We tend to see such control as essential to the meaning, value and purpose of our being. How much of the compulsive workaholism of our activities serves to authenticate ourselves as persons (to ourselves and others) and to prove that we have value, meaning and purpose in the world! To put it simply, we live as though our doing determined our being."[33]

Focus is *a single-minded devotion to and enduring pursuit of God*. It involves eliminating things and activities from your life that distract you from being who God created you to be and redirecting your energy toward accomplishing His will for your life. In the midst of our frenzied lives today, God calls us to move from busyness to focus. If you are caught in a lifestyle of busyness, you can practice several spiritual disciplines to reverse this unhealthy behavior and regain your equilibrium. God will use these small things to shape you into Christ's image. Try one or more of these disciplines to help quiet your soul, slow your pace, and refocus your life on God.

Maintaining Focus by Unplugging

If it has an on/off switch, I own it. I love gadgets. My favorite device is my Smartphone. I don't know what I'd do without my smartphone. It keeps me plugged in to the world, no matter where I am or what I'm doing.

That's the problem. Although my smartphone brings the world to me, it also pushes those closest to me further away. Forget about all the superhero power smartphones possesses; even an ordinary cell phone takes priority over just about everything else.

People often say, "Excuse me" in the middle of an important conversation to answer their phones. Before cell phones a person could get away and enjoy time alone to think and reflect or could enjoy a cup of coffee and good conversation with a friend. Now forget about it. The phone rings and demands center stage in its owner's life.

A few years ago, Susan and I dined in a restaurant with a good friend in La Jolla, California. Sam and I have been through a lot together. As the chairperson of the personnel committee at a former church, he had labored to see that my family was well cared for. He had gone through some difficult days while he was at the church, and I had done my best to care for his soul. In the process of caring for each other, we had become good friends. Without going into detail now, I can say that Sam's suffering came nearer to the suffering of Job than any man I've ever known (see chap. 4). He had lost everything, but God had restored Sam's wealth. A few years ago, celebrating God's faithfulness over a meal in South Carolina, we had talked about how God had restored him, just as he had restored Job. What we hadn't talked about is that God hadn't restored Sam's family. Every time I thought about Sam after that, had prayed that God would restore his family.

God was gracious. We hadn't driven to La Jolla just to see Sam; we had gone to meet his new wife, Kathy. In the middle of dinner my smartphone vibrated, and I picked it up to respond to the text message. It got quiet at the table. When I realized how rude I had been, I turned off the phone and put it away. The compulsion to remain plugged in annihilates the possibility of retreating from life's slow grind. The text message was trivial; yet I had allowed it to take precedence over what should have had my undivided attention.

There is a reason these devices have an on/off switch. Turning them off is often a good choice. Like other spiritual disciplines, unplugging is a small thing; but it might just be the most important thing I can do to stop feeding my compulsion toward busyness. Thomas writes, "The sin many of us fall into is not that we shake our fists at God and defy Him to His face; that is the sin of unbelievers. Our sin is that we passively rebel against God, filling our lives with so much noise and busyness that God's voice cannot, or will not, penetrate."[34]

Unplugging—*a planned respite from constant connection to the world*—is a small thing Christians can do to reduce the noise around them and prepare to listen to God's voice. I'm working to find the on/off switch on my smartphone more often. During our vacation this year, I turned it off and went a full week without checking voice mail or e-mail. When we returned, I found myself less compulsive about always being plugged in.

Maintaining Focus Through Silence

Silence is more than the absence of noise. It is removing distractions to recalibrate your soul to God's heartbeat. In 2004 a piano tuner requested that the operators of the nearby 1,120-megawatt Sima power plant shut down operations for nine hours so that he could tune a grand piano located in a huge underground hall. The piano tuner could not tune the instrument with the constant hum of hydroelectric generators distracting him. The concert hall, located inside a mountain in the scenic Hardanger Fjord in western Norway, is renowned for its acoustic properties. The senior vice president at Norwegian Power Company, Tron Engelbrethensen, says this was the first time they had to shut down production to tune a piano; but they complied with the request because, as he said, "When you put a big piano in there, you also need to tune it and that is very difficult if the machines are running."[35] In the same way, busyness keeps people from hearing from God. The Bible says, "Be silent in the presence of the Lord GOD, for the Day of the LORD is near. Indeed, the LORD has prepared a sacrifice; He has consecrated His guests." (Zephaniah 1:7)

I always look forward to teaching the proclamation and worship seminar with my mentor, Gary McCoy. He brings deep spirituality and passion for spiritual formation into the classroom. At a recent seminar on our Pacific Northwest campus, he introduced our participants to a Benedictine meal, a simple meal—in this case a bologna sandwich—eaten in total silence. Most of the time I rush through meals, working while I eat or paying more attention to the conversation than the food.

This time in the silence I savored the food and the company. It was amazing how connected I felt to those in the room and how silence seasoned the experience.

Actually, I'm no stranger to silence. With the slip of a surgeon's scalpel in 1996, I lost the ability to speak. My world crashed in around me. As weeks became months, I drifted into depression and was losing hope. It wasn't the cancer—my prognosis was good—it was the thought that without a voice, I was useless to God, my church, and my family that paralyzed me. As Robert Mulholland Jr. says, "We tend to evaluate our own meaning, value and purpose, as well as those of others, not by the quality of our being but by what we do and how effectively we do it."[36] I had fallen into the performance trap. It was beginning to look as though I would never preach again.

Then on January 29, 1997, after almost a year of silence, God restored my voice and extended my ministry. And I am grateful. Every year on the anniversary of that date, I honor the Lord with a speech fast to help me remember. I remember that my sermons should be God's words, not mine. I remember that without His power I wouldn't have a voice to speak them. I remember that God's people are good. His church did not turn its back on me but supported me through my trial. I remember Claude Cone, the denominational executive who made sure my pulpit was filled while I recuperated, at no cost to our church. I remember Robbie, my colleague, who rubbed baby oil on my son when worry made him break out in hives on the night of my surgery. I remember the Sunday School class that paid for my airplane ticket to receive the surgery. I remember Dr. Netterville, of the Vanderbilt Voice Clinic, who performed the surgery that gave me back my voice. I remember that God cares. I remember that even in my darkest moment, God was there. I will never forget the touch of His unseen hand on my soul.

I've come to look forward to my annual speech fast. Not talking really isn't that hard. With so much to remember and be grateful for, I don't have time to talk anyway. For me, silence for a day takes on special meaning; but beyond the special significance it holds for me, it allows me to observe and reflect on life without the constant need to provide commentary on what is happening. It awakens my awareness of what God is doing around me.

Whether the silence lasts a day or an hour, it clears the clutter to allow Christians to hear the voice of God. The Bible says, "Be still, and know that I *am* God: I will be exalted among the heathen, I will be exalted in the earth." Psalm 46:10 (KJV)

Henri Nouwen writes, "In our chatty world, in which the word has lost its power to communicate, silence helps us to keep our mind and heart anchored in the future world and allows us to speak from there a creative and recreative word to the present world."[37] In reality, we don't have anything to say unless we are willing to stop speaking to hear from God

Maintaining Focus Through Solitude

Gary Thomas calls diversions a drug that keeps us from entering God's presence. He writes, "A drug addict cannot expect to give up drugs without paying the price of withdrawal. We who have been drugged by diversions cannot expect to enter the quiet without a struggle. Our souls will roar for diversion, the fix that saves us from God's presence."[38]

Solitude is more than being alone; it is a distraction-free environment to slow down and listen to God. The Bible shows that people who walk closely with God often practice the discipline of solitude. For example, after the Hebrew people had been captured and taken to Babylon, King Darius issued an edict declaring that anyone who was caught praying to anyone except the king would be thrown into the lions' den. Among the Hebrew exiles was Daniel, a godly man who had found favor with the king.

Talk about spiritual discipline! Daniel was accustomed to being alone with God and praying three times a day. When adversity came, he sought God's presence as he had always done before.

Jesus spent 40 days and nights in solitude to prepare for His temptation (see Matt. 4:1), and Saul spent three days in darkness prior to discovering his life mission (see Acts 9:9). Solitude prepared and shaped these men for the unique ministries God had for them.

Jesus often found it necessary to withdraw from the activities of ministry to spend time alone with His Father. For example, after a busy period of teaching, healing, and casting out demons, Jesus went out to "a deserted place" (see Luke 4:42). Luke 6:12 says Jesus "went out to the mountain to pray and spent all night in prayer to God" before choosing the 12 disciples. Luke 21:37 records that Jesus spent the days teaching in the temple, "but in the evening He would go out and spend the night on what is called the Mount of Olives." Jesus maintained a habit of solitude with His Father.

Maintaining Focus Through Rest

Elijah wasn't afraid to take on the prophets of Baal at Mount Carmel, but he ran scared from the threats of a single woman—Jezebel (see 1 Kings 19:3). She was no ordinary woman; she was evil to the bone. He ran for a day, then sat down under a broom tree and told the Lord he was ready to die. He had had enough. As far as he was concerned, he was the only person left alive who was faithful to God and had not bowed his knee to Baal.

In an instant despair swallowed Mount Carmel's victory and Elijah was ready to give up. Fatigued, Elijah rested. Then an angel of the Lord woke him and gave him something to eat. Elijah slept again, and the angel woke him again, giving him more food and drink. Only after he regained his strength did Elijah begin the 40-day journey to the mountain of the Lord and stand in the presence of God. The Lord wasn't in the mighty wind that devastated the mountain; neither was he in the earthquake or in the fire that followed. The Lord was in the understated, still, small voice. Elijah was about to enter his rest; but before he did, God had a few things he needed him to do. He needed him to anoint a new king and dedicate Elisha to continue his work. Elijah obeyed, and God translated him into heaven— his final rest (see 2 Kings 2:11).

It doesn't surprise me that Elijah was depressed after his great victory against the prophets of Baal. After the rush of ministry fades, depression often creeps in. Neither does it surprise me that Elijah became afraid even after seeing the cataclysmic display of God's power at Mount Carmel. Fatigue often produces faltering faith. Elijah was human. He could only do so much; he had expended all his energy.

Under the broom tree Elijah found rest. At the hand of an angel he found nourishment. God did not create people with the ability to run without resting. Strength comes from waiting on the Lord (see Isa. 40:31), not from depending on human resources.

Rest is a part of God's good plan. After six days of labor God paused from His creative activities to rest. The Bible says, "God blessed the seventh day and declared it holy, for on it He rested from His work of creation" (Gen. 2:3). The period of rest completed the creation, thus sanctifying it and making it a holy day. God calls His people to imitate His rest in the fourth commandment: "Remember to dedicate the Sabbath day: You are to labor six days and do all your work, but the seventh day is a Sabbath to the LORD your God. You must not do any work—you, your son or daughter, your male or female slave, your livestock, or the foreigner who is within your gates" (Ex. 20:8-10).

Today Christians typically honor Sunday as the Lord's Day, reserving this day for worship, rest, and acts of spiritual devotion. Sabbath rest is more than a cessation of labor. It is an opportunity to remember what life's purpose is and to renew a spirit of trust in God. It is a conscious choice to submit to God. Rest is God's good gift to His people. Remembering to rest is His people's good gift back to God. It is one way we show utter dependence on Him and take time to develop intimacy with Him.

The disciplines of unplugging, silence, solitude, and Sabbath rest slow down the hands of busyness as they race around the clock. They open up the hearts of those who practice them to live their lives at a reflective, intentional pace. These disciplines are small things Christians intentionally do to open themselves to God's work of conforming them to the image of Christ. Practicing them paces life. They slow us down and enable us to accomplish more of what God wants us to do by doing less of everything else. After all, how can we know what to do if we never listen to God?

CHAPTER 4 FROM DESPAIR TO HOPE

The Bible says, "There is ... a time to mourn and a time to dance" (Eccl. 3:1-4), Have you ever thought about how those two experiences might relate to each other? Hope is the path that connects mourning and rejoicing. No matter how rocky or winding or lonely that path seems, be assured that God is with you every step of the way. He knows about your pain. He cares about your pain. And He is with you in the pain. He wants you to feel free to cry out to Him honestly and passionately about what you are experiencing and then to invite Him into your grief. When you experience His presence in your pain, you are on the path of hope. Four spiritual disciplines will help you find your way.

THE SHADOW OF DEATH

Terry, Maria, and Zach were living lives straight out of a Norman Rockwell painting. It wasn't that life had always been easy for them; it hadn't. Terry was an Air Force pilot who had flown in and out of dangerous places all over the world, but all of that was in their rearview mirror. In six months, they would move to their final duty station, where Terry would pilot a desk until his retirement; but before they moved, Maria would deliver their second child—a girl. They decided to name her Zoe, a Greek name meaning life *or* energy.[39] In preparation for Zoe's birth, Maria cleared her calendar, handed over all her outside commitments to others, designed the perfect nursery, and stocked up on everything pink. She had planned everything down to the last detail, accounting for every contingency. Well, almost every one.

It was supposed to be the last visit before the delivery date. They were just going to check her weight; take her blood pressure; and of course, listen to the heartbeat.

It was supposed to be a routine visit, one more thing to check off the list—just another errand to run in preparation for the big day.

A few days later, Terry and Maria gathered up the strength to do the impossible—they went to the hospital to deliver their little girl, whose heart had stopped beating.

Just as summer follows spring and Christmas follows Thanksgiving, death follows life. The seasons of life bring order out of chaos and sense to the slow ticking of the clock. The Bible says, "There is an occasion for everything, and a time for every activity under heaven: a time to give birth and a time to die; a time to plant and a time to uproot" (Eccl. 3:1-2). No one wonders why people

74

in their 80s die. Death is a sense of completion to those lives. Death makes perfect sense then. Death is just part of life's rhythm, another season, another celestial tick of the clock. That's the way it's supposed to be. People should die after they've lived a full life. Zoe's death, on the other hand, made no sense. She died before she took her first breath. It made no sense. It didn't follow order; it was out of season. Without any sense of equilibrium, Terry and Maria grieved; looked toward heaven; and asked, "Why?"

"There is an occasion for everything and a time for every activity under heaven: a time to give birth and a time to die; a time to plant and a time to uproot." (Ecclesiastes 3:1-2)

Numb from their loss, Terry and Maria stumbled into the hospital seven weeks later for a "cut, look, repeat" procedure on a squamous cell carcinoma patch on Terry's skin. With Terry's cancer history they both had some concern, but neither of them thought it was as serious as the melanoma doctors had removed 10 years before. It was supposed to take an hour. The clock ticked until time stood still. After five times of cutting and looking under the microscope to see if it was all gone, Terry called for Maria. "Promise me you will marry again. Find Zach a Christian dad," Terry said. Maria didn't want to answer. She was still throbbing from Zoe's funeral. She couldn't process this nightmare. But not wanting to argue with him, she answered, "I promise."

Maria collapsed in the waiting room. She lost all feeling. She didn't know if she could depend on anything, not even gravity. "I was spiraling, knowing I would soon feel cold death on my husband, just as I had on my daughter," Maria says. "I was losing my breath, my movement, my speech."

On the seventh cut Terry was in the clear.

Five months later, after they had already said good-bye to everyone, Maria went to see the doctor who had delivered Zoe for him to release her to a new ob-gyn at her new duty station. Yes, by the grace of God she was pregnant again. This time she was 20 weeks along. Terry waited with their household goods, which were boxed and stacked on their front lawn, while Maria left for a quick trip to the doctor. Then she would rejoin Terry, supervise the movers, and begin their two-week vacation. She had every detail planned. They would stay near national parks all the way across the country, soaking in God's beautiful creation. After what they had been through, they deserved it. If anybody deserved it, Terry and Maria did.

While Terry was waiting for the movers, Maria called. "Honey, they can't find a heartbeat. Can you come down here?" Maria said through her tears. When Terry arrived, the doctor began searching for the heartbeat again. There was none. Terry collapsed in the chair. Instead of leaving for their vacation, they headed to a larger hospital for another medical procedure. Just when they thought they couldn't handle any more grief, it deluged them.

THE BEST-LAID PLANS

When it came time to retire, Sam Varner's choices were wide open. He could afford to live almost anywhere, but he and his new bride chose Carmel Valley, California. The central coast of California is breathtaking, and its climate is moderate; but Carmel Valley is the location of choice for those who prefer the typical day to be in the mid 70s instead of the high 60s. Not many people get to retire in their 40s; Varner was one of the lucky ones. But really, *luck,* isn't the right word to describe Varner's life. He had worked hard to get where he was. Varner was a winner.

Varner was a strength-and-conditioning coach for Clemson University when they won the national championship in 1981-82 and the 1982 Orange Bowl. He also coached athletes in the 1988, 1992, and 1994 winter Olympics. His client list included Bill Johnson, Debbie Armstrong, Picabo Street, and Tommy Moe, who all took home gold, and Hilary Lindh, Kyle Rasmussen, and Diann Roffe, who won silver medals. During those years Varner had parlayed his earnings into a substantial nest egg by playing the options and futures market, and now he was ready to enjoy the good life.

Everything changed on October 27, 1997. In Hong Kong the Hang Seng Index fell, and the Japanese Nikkei dropped 2 percent, setting off a chain reaction around the world. London's FTSE 100 Index dropped 2 percent; and the Dow Jones Industrial Average, NASDAQ, and S&P 500 plummeted. After falling 350 points, the Dow halted trading for 30 minutes. When it resumed, it continued falling until trading ended early at 3:35 p.m. This minicrash resulted in the Dow's suffering the biggest percentage loss to that point in recorded stock-market history[40] and in Varner's losing everything.

Varner should have shifted his money into asset-preservation funds, but he says, "I got greedy and wanted shortcut ways of making more money, so I started buying options, which are riskier. You can make more money, but you can also lose more." Varner wasn't accustomed to losing. He had spent his life being a winner, working with winners, and helping winners win more. To Varner, this was just a setback. All it meant was that he would have to go back to work—-a blessing in disguise, really.

Instead of going back into coaching, Varner decided he would write a book. He didn't know anything about the publishing business; but it couldn't be that hard, right? He didn't write a query letter; he didn't do any market research; he didn't write a book proposal—he just starting writing. Two years later when he finished the manuscript, he found an agent and waited for the phone to ring. Believe it or not, it did.

"I've got great news for you," Varner's agent said. "A major publisher wants to buy your manuscript!" That was good news. Varner was dead broke. He was ready to cash a paycheck. "There's only one catch," the agent continued. "They want you to take out all the Christian stuff from the book."

Varner had a choice to make. He could edit out his Christian values and cash a check for the huge advance they had promised; but in doing so, he would be selling out. When the long-awaited call came, Varner said, "No thank you" and turned down the money.

He lost the book deal, but he kept his integrity and knew that the God who gave him the passion to spread his message of good health would provide a publisher for him. It was a dark day, a day of testing, but a day that ushered in a stronger resolve and passion.

Varner's agent called him again, this time with better news. Element Books wanted to make *Slimmer, Younger, Stronger* their lead book in 2000 and wanted to release it in hardback in the United States, Great Britain, Australia, and Canada. The advance was good; but better still, they were going to sponsor a national tour to help Varner promote the book. Things were looking up.

However, after only one stop the publisher *pulled* the plug on the tour and gave Varner some bad news: it was declaring bankruptcy. The advance was all the money Varner would see.

Varner's drive and determination remained intact. He didn't just have a message; he had a passion. Just as he had helped elite athletes in the past, he wanted to help the masses gain optimal physical health; so he pressed on. The Pebble Beach Corporation hired him as its fitness director and promised to help him launch his fitness program on a national scale. With the prestige of the Pebble Beach name behind him, Varner believed this would be his big break. He worked at finding investors, tweaking his program, and developing a business plan that included new books and infomercials. All was on track. The timing was right. Then hijacked airplanes hit the twin towers in New York. Subsequently, Varner's investors pulled out.

Varner didn't quit. Winners never do. He pressed on, working as a personal trainer while he beat the pavement trying to line up new investors. He held on to the small thread of hope that remained as he tried to restart the momentum necessary to secure investors and launch a national fitness program. Life was getting more difficult as Varner struggled to keep his family together. A point came when his wife had had enough. Saying she didn't want to live like this anymore, she walked out the door, never to return. Soon after, the president of Pebble Beach died, and Varner's dreams died with him. He had lost his fortune. He had lost his wife. He was losing hope.

"I began to feel like Job. I really did. There was one point when I basically had nothing." Varner says. "I was penniless."

THE SUFFERING OF JOB

When Varner identified with Job, he wasn't just using a
figure of speech. Job, once a very prosperous man, lost all
of his wealth, his children, and his health. As he scraped his
sores with broken pottery, lamented his losses, and listened
to the poor counsel of his friends, Job remained faithful to
God. He said, "Though he slay me, yet will I trust in him"
(Job 13:15, KJV). Where does that kind of faith come
from? How could Job lose everything yet refuse to shake
his fist toward heaven and curse God?

All Job had left were his wife and his so-called
friends. Yet he never cursed God.

Job's wife wasn't much help. She advised him to
curse God and die; but Job responded by asking, "Should
we accept only good from God and not adversity?" (Job
2:10).

Job's friends weren't helpful either. But to their
credit, at least they came to him in his hour of need. They
performed a wonderful ministry for Job. For seven days
and seven nights, they sat with him and said nothing,
because they "saw that his suffering was very intense." (Job
2:13). Now that's friendship. They sat beside their friend
and entered his suffering.

After a while, Job began to grieve aloud, prompting
his friends' response. They would have been better off
remaining silent and listening to Job. Instead, they decided
their friend didn't need their support; rather, he needed a
lesson in theology.

Job and his friends argued and argued. While Job
was a righteous man and claimed he had done nothing to
deserve this treatment, his friends in effect said, "Of course
you have. God wouldn't be doing this to you unless you

deserved it." Like skillful prosecutors, each of them took his turn accusing this righteous man of sinning and getting what he deserved. Job continued to defend himself until God set the record straight. "After the LORD had finished speaking to Job, He said to Eliphaz the Temanite: 'I am angry with you and your two friends, for you have not spoken the truth about Me, as My servant Job has' " (Job 42:7).

The common theology in Job's day was that God played favorites. He prospered those who honored Him and zapped those who didn't. Because Job had lived righteously all his life, he couldn't understand why God wasn't shining His favor on him or, more to the point, why God was doing quite the opposite. It appeared that God had turned His back on Job altogether.

Job's wife and friends were no help; and frankly, at the time, Job didn't feel that God was on his side either. He felt forsaken. He wanted to have a hearing before God.

He wanted to make the point that he was living righteously and if he was wrong, he wanted God to tell him he was wrong. Job knew he couldn't drag God into court to settle the matter. He said, "If it is a matter of power, look, He is the Mighty One! If it is a matter of justice, who can summon Him?" (Job 9:19).

FINDING HOPE IN CHRIST

Varner thought about suicide but just couldn't do that to his family. He had hit rock bottom; he had nothing left and nowhere to turn. That's when he called me. "I'm trying to do everything right. I go to church. I don't know what else to do." Varner said. Prayerfully, I listened as he told me the details of his trial. When he finished, he asked, "What do you think about all of this, Pastor?"

"Sam, 1 think this is your finest hour," I said.

"Jim, did you just hear me? I've lost everything—my wife, my money. I've lost everything!" He replied, "Yes, I heard you. Sam, I still think this is your finest hour. In fact, I envy you. Right now God is all you have; soon you will know that He is what you need the most."

In the crucible of suffering, it is easy to give up, and some people do. They give in to discouragement, blaming God for their predicament. Others respond by inviting God into their pain and thereby experience His presence in a deeper, more meaningful way than ever before. Because Jesus Christ dwells in you, hope is available. You can experience His presence in difficult times by practicing the spiritual disciplines of lament, confession, celebration, and praise.

Finding Hope in Christ Through Lament

Job had nowhere to turn. There was no place where he could have his day in court and no one to stand beside him. He had nothing. He had no one. Job was alone.

No, Job wasn't alone. God was there. Earlier Job had said, "Naked I came from my mother's womb, and naked I will leave this life. The LORD gives, and the LORD takes away. Praise the name of Yahweh." (Job 1:21). God remains during good times and bad. He is there in times of plenty and need. Even when he had nothing, Job was content and blessed the name of the Lord.

Job's suffering wasn't punishment. His trials brought glory to God and served an eternal purpose. Even though Job didn't know the purpose, he remained faithful to God. God wasn't picking on Job or punishing him but was allowing Job to suffer to prove to Satan that Job's righteousness didn't evoke God's blessings. In other words, even if God removed His outward blessings from him, Job wouldn't forsake God.

Instead of turning his back on God, Job lamented— he invited God into his sorrow and experienced His presence in the depths of his pain. From his lament burst forth praise. Even after experiencing the helpless, desperate plight of the human condition, Job blessed the name of the Lord.

I knew Varner, like Job, was facing a defining moment, a testing through fire that would shape his soul. I knew God wouldn't forsake him, and I knew he was about to experience the comfort that comes from pressing into God. I encouraged Varner to lament, inviting God into his sorrow. As he did, he learned that he didn't need the things he had lost; he needed God. In the midst of this trial, Varner learned what was valuable to him. It wasn't what he lost. It was what he couldn't lose—his relationship with God.

This was Varner's finest hour because he was desperate for God. It wasn't riches, comfort, or security he longed for anymore. He wanted God. He wanted to know God was there and cared for him. If nothing else, suffering is a time when we learn to long for God—to be desperate for Him.

Lament erupted from Varner's core as he poured out his soul to the Lord. It is easier to be in control than out of control. It is easier to live with the illusion that everything is OK. But it wasn't. Varner was living in an evil world where bad things happen, even to good people. That wasn't going to change. Through these trials he learned he couldn't stop the bad, but that didn't mean he couldn't pursue his good God through lament.

During his finest hour, Varner stopped asking for God's blessings and started asking for God's presence. Through lament, he emptied himself of his ambitions, preferences, uniqueness, idiosyncrasies, pride, and abilities. In his emptiness, he found room to encounter God. Then he was ready to invite God into his sorrow.

Eight months later one of Varner's colleagues from the Olympics called to see if he would be interested in working in South Carolina with a developer who wanted to incorporate wellness into the communities he was building. Today Varner is implementing his wellness program and doesn't have financial worries. Just as God did with Job, He took care of Varner. Several years ago when he returned to California for a friend's wedding, I asked him to speak at the church I served. After telling the story about his finest hour, he gave the following advice: "Love God with all your heart and always be thankful in whatever situation you are in, whether you are rich, poor, strong, healthy, or sick. Always be thankful. Also trust Him. You don't know what's ahead, but the Lord does. Trust Him to take care of you. Obey Him. He cares more about you than you could ever imagine. So stay true to the Lord." Varner added, "My greatest accomplishment in life is my relationship with God. That's what has real meaning."

Varner found satisfaction, not in the restoration of his wealth but in the deepening of his relationship with God. That is always the case when we press into God in our time of despair. The loss that prompts your sorrow opens your heart in a new and fresh way to usher in the presence of God — not to fix the pain or solve the problem but just to be there. Michael Card writes, "The ultimate answer to all laments is not to be found in the specifics of what is lamented for. The true answer for a lament of disease is not ultimately a cure. The real solution for a lament of financial distress is never simply money. The answer is always found

84

in the Presence of God. It is rarely what we ask for, but it is always what we ultimately need."[41]

Years have passed since Terry and Maria lost Zoe. Terry has been through one more "cut, look, repeat" cancer operation. Their son Zach had surgery for a life-threatening tumor in his ear. They lost another child during pregnancy, their fourth loss. But by God's grace they have two more children now—Gabe and Cecilia.

Maria knows the song of lament. She's sung all of the verses and the chorus many times. With loss stacked on loss, she invited God into her sorrow and found Him to be faithful. "After Zoe's death I was sure of the definitive existence of God," Maria says.

"He woke me from a sleep that was not restful. He patiently forced air into and out of my lungs when I did not want to breathe. He moved me out of bed when all I wanted was a quiet coffin of my own to escape the immeasurable grief. He gave me tears to wash the pain from my eyes. And so He began the rest of my life on this planet without Zoe." "Sleep is restful," Maria continues. "I can take a deep breath of air and slowly let it out. I can get myself out of bed every morning. There is taste in food again. There are more tears of joy than of grief. God is good. I could not face this world without Him. Everything in this world, in this life, on this planet is more than I can handle. God constantly lets me know I cannot do it without Him. He is God. The happy ending is not that I have other children and my husband lived. The happy ending is that I have God."

It seems that contemporary Christianity has decided to bypass lament and go straight to celebration. Bruce Demarest writes, "Our attempts at worship often seem better suited to entertainment than ushering worshipers into God's awesome and holy presence."[42]

What's missing? Lament.

How can creatures praise their Creator without lamenting their fallen state? A whole book of the Bible, Lamentations, is dedicated to lament, along with two-thirds of the ancient hymnal, the Book of Psalms.[43]Yet almost all of the worship services I've attended in my lifetime have feasted on praise while starving the people of lament. Even most funerals have become life celebrations instead of a time to mourn.

Richard Beck writes, "If a church has not been raised on both praise and lament it will be ill-equipped to provide its members with the words to articulate the full range of human experience."[44]In Lamentations, the prophet Jeremiah mourned the destruction of Jerusalem by the Babylonians. In the middle of his long lament, Jeremiah cried: "My soul has been deprived of peace; I have forgotten what happiness is. (18) Then I thought: My future is lost, as well as my hope from the LORD." (Lamentations 3:17-18)

But then came a pivotal turning point in Jeremiah's grief: "Because of the LORD's faithful love we do not perish, for His mercies never end. (23) They are new every morning; great is Your faithfulness! (24) I say: The LORD is my portion, therefore I will put my hope in Him." (Lamentations 3:22-24)

Jeremiah laid his soul bare before God in stanza after stanza of agonizing grief. Yet in the end, his lament gave way to hope in the Lord. Authentic lament leads to a sense of dependence on God, fosters a spirit of confession of sin, and ushers in celebration and praise.

Even if worship planners at your church don't include lament in the order of worship, you can. Whether it is during the pastor's prayer, the reading of Scripture, or the singing of a hymn, take time to invite God into your sorrow. Acknowledge His presence in the midst of your pain and invite Him to be with you, whether or not He removes the pain.

Finding Hope in Christ Through Confession

Lament prepares the heart for general and specific confession. In general, worshipers confess their humanity, finiteness, and frailty. In specific, they confess their sins.

King David was a strong man—a leader of men. He was a spiritual man who wrote many beautiful psalms that worshipers sang in his day and read today. Yet David had a severe moral lapse. It was the time of year when kings lead their troops to war, but David was nowhere to be found. Instead of assuming his leadership role, he lingered around the palace. While walking around the roof, he spotted a beautiful woman taking a bath. Instead of turning his head and walking away, he stayed and watched. Later he sent for her and consummated his sin with her in the palace. When she became pregnant, David tried to cover up his sin but to no avail. Ultimately, his sin led to the murder of the woman's husband.

David knew he had sinned against God; but after this conversation with Nathan, the weight of his sin sank in. David didn't try to shift the blame or avoid responsibility; instead, he confessed his sin to God. By confessing his sin, David submitted to God's judgment and discovered God's mercy. God punished David. His sin cost him his son and his reputation; but in the midst of God's judgment, grace flowed. God forgave David's sin (see 2 Sam. 12:13b).

God forgave David's sin and extended grace to him. This is the power of confession. In the midst of confession, God's grace flows and gives us what we don't deserve— forgiveness. His mercy falls down on us and doesn't give us what we deserve—death.

In this moment, you are in the presence of a holy God who knows about your sin. You could try to shift the blame or avoid responsibility, but you know He knows about your sin; so instead, confess your sins to Him. As a sin comes to mind, say, 'Yes, God, You re right. That's sin." Take a moment now to name your sins to God. Admit them. Confess them. Repent of them, no matter how small you may think they are. Use Psalm 51 as a guide for your prayer of confession.

Read Psalm 51:3. Just as David did, admit your sinfulness before God.

Read Psalm 51:1-2. Ask God to forgive you of your sin and to show mercy to you. Ask Him to cleanse you of your sin.

Read Psalm 51:10 and invite God to change your life.

Read Psalm 51:12 and ask God to return the joy of His salvation to you.

Confession needs to be a daily discipline. It is so much more than just tacking "and forgive me of all my sins" onto the end of a prayer. It is allowing sinfulness to break your heart, just as it breaks the heart of God. 1 John 1:9 promises that God will forgive those who confess their sins to him: "If we confess our sins, He is faithful and righteous to forgive us our sins and to cleanse us from all unrighteousness." Practicing the spiritual discipline of confession means keeping a short sin list. As soon as you sin, confess it to God, and He will forgive you. You will find that the act of confession will help take you from despair over your sinfulness to hope in God's grace.

Finding Hope in Christ Through Celebration

Lament provides a context for heartfelt celebration. Just look at the life of Joseph. Out of jealousy over Joseph's favored relationship with their dad, Joseph's brothers tore his robe off him, soiled it with the blood of an animal, and threw him into a pit. Showing the garment of favoritism to their father, they deceived him by telling him Joseph was dead. But Joseph wasn't dead. His brothers had sold him as a slave to a caravan. In the beginning, Egypt wasn't that bad for Joseph. Sure, he missed his father and longed for home, but he had a good assignment. He did well for himself and became the head of the entire household. Potiphar didn't keep anything from him except, of course, his wife. Potiphar's wife had another idea. Finding Joseph attractive, she attempted to seduce him.

She wouldn't take no for an answer. She clutched Joseph and demanded that he sleep with her. Joseph didn't. Instead, he turned and ran. As he ran from the seductress's grasp, his clothes tore. Once again, Joseph sat in a "pit"—a prison cell—with his clothes in someone else's hand. His boss' wife used his clothes as a garment of accusation to deceive her husband into thinking Joseph had tried to seduce her. Potiphar threw Joseph into prison.

Joseph may have thought he had lost it all. How could he know God would use him to preserve Egypt and his family through a time of famine? At the time, perhaps he thought he had nothing. Nothing except his integrity and his faith. But then again, whether you live in Pharaoh's palace or in a prison, what else is there? Joseph had more than his integrity; he had God's favor. God gave him the ability to interpret the dreams of the baker and the cupbearer when they were in prison. Two years later the cupbearer advised Pharaoh to send for Joseph to interpret two troubling dreams. Joseph interpreted the dreams and suggested that Pharaoh appoint a wise man to administer a savings plan during the seven years of plenty to provide for the nation during the seven years of drought to follow.

Pharaoh followed his advice and appointed Joseph to prepare the country for their future. He put his signet ring on Joseph's hand and a garment of exaltation on his back. Life progressed just as Joseph predicted. There were seven years of plenty in the land until drought swallowed the prosperity the Egyptians were enjoying. But because of Joseph, there was still bread in Egypt. He had stored a portion of the grain, preparing for difficult days.

Nine years after Joseph ascended to power, he saw his brothers again. Joseph's brothers, who had thrown him into the pit and had sold him into slavery, stood before him asking for grain. Joseph recognized them, but they didn't recognize him. Right away Joseph accused them of spying and threw them in prison. Three days later he released all but one of them, gave them the grain they requested, and even returned their money to them. He kept one of the brothers in jail to guarantee they would return with Benjamin, the brother they told Joseph was still at home with their aged father. When they returned home, Israel refused to let Benjamin go to Egypt to secure the release of his other son.

But when they ran out of food—and options—Israel agreed to send Benjamin. This time Joseph had a meal prepared for his brothers and instructed his stewards to give them the grain they needed and to insert his special cup into Benjamin's bag. Soon after they left for home, Joseph sent his men to intercept them; search through their bags for his cup; and when they found it, to accuse them of stealing and bring them back to him.

Joseph had them right where he wanted them. His plan was to throw Benjamin in jail so that his father would come to Egypt to get him. Then Joseph could reunite with his father before he died. What Joseph didn't count on was an impassioned plea by Judah to put him in jail instead of Benjamin so that the sorrow wouldn't kill his father. For the third time Joseph broke down, but this time, it was in front of his brothers. The first time Joseph had overheard the brothers lamenting what they had done to him. When Joseph heard their contrition, he went into a private chamber and wept. Joseph had wept a second time when he saw his younger brother Benjamin. Again, he went into a private chamber and wept. This time Joseph didn't hide his passion from his brothers. He sent his attendants from the room, but he wept so loud that they heard him. Revealing himself to his brothers, he said, "And now don't be worried or angry with yourselves for selling me here, because God sent me ahead of you to preserve life. (Gen. 45:5). Joseph gave them wagons to carry their food and fresh garments for their back—garments of reconciliation—and sent them back to get their father so that they could live in Egypt and avoid the five years of famine to come.

The brothers did as Joseph said, and Joseph and his father were reunited. Israel and his family settled in the land of Goshen, where God provided for the children of Israel through the famine and beyond. Israel lived out his life near his favored son, Joseph—the young dreamer who became a ruler. Father and son alike celebrated. Celebration came but only after tears.

As you lament, you will grieve; but you can experience good grief. Your tears don't have to be laced with despair. As you invite God into your sorrow, you will experience His presence. Don't try to replace the tears with celebration. Instead, let them usher in the celebration. God is a good God; His mercy endures forever. You will see that vivid truth when your tears blur your vision. Sorrow may last through the night, but hope follows the mourning.

Finding Hope in Christ Through Praise

Lament gives way to praise. The Bible says to give thanks "always for everything to God the Father in the name of our Lord Jesus Christ" (Eph. 5:20). Easier said than done.

Because God would not listen to reason, Jonah the prophet thought he had to run. As he put it, he was running "from the presence of the LORD" (Jonah 1:3). He boarded a ship in Joppa headed toward Tarshish, a Phoenician city on the southern coast of Spain—the opposite direction from Nineveh. God had instructed Jonah to go to the Far East. In his rebellion, Jonah chose to do the exact opposite and go to the distant west.

Aboard the ship, Jonah was fast asleep, believing he had escaped God's control. He was wrong. His shipmates awoke him to tell him he hadn't. There was a storm at sea. Not just any storm. It was a storm that brought terror to the normally fearless crew. The all-powerful, all-knowing God, whom Jonah described as the "LORD God of heaven who made the sea and the dry land" (Jonah 1:9), hurled a great wind on the sea that caused a great storm. The crew believed there was a good chance that the ship would be lost. To lighten the load, they jettisoned the cargo. When that wasn't enough, they fell on their knees and started praying to their gods. The captain of the ship awoke Jonah and asked him to do the same. Meanwhile, the crew cast lots to see who was to blame for the lost cargo and their imminent doom. The lots fell on Jonah. The crew threw Jonah overboard, and the seas calmed. It appeared that it was over for Jonah, but it wasn't.

Even in his darkest moment God was still there.

God appointed a fish to swallow Jonah. In all probability Jonah didn't view the fish as God's grace, but it was. The fish was not punishment; it was a biological submarine prepared by God to sustain Jonah's life. In the beginning, I'm sure Jonah was frustrated because he had lost total control of the situation. So he prayed to the Lord.

In his prayer Jonah blamed God for his troubles (see Jonah 2:3 -4), and he complained about his trials (see Jonah 2:5-6). Life couldn't be much worse for Jonah. He was so low that he was at the "roots of the mountains" (Jonah 2:6 KJV), a poetic way of referring to the bottom of the ocean.

After his lament, Jonah had a dramatic change in attitude; he remembered that God is in control (see Jonah 2:6-7). This time he didn't rebel against that fact. It comforted him. Today was pressing in on him so hard that yesterday was but a faint memory, and tomorrow had no significance. Jonah was living in the now. At last, he was taking life one day at a time, trusting in God. God took care of Jonah. Jonah had nowhere to run and nowhere to hide. Even when he had tried to outrun God, had conspired with others to try to out row God, and had found himself in the belly of the fish, Jonah rested in the palm of God's hand—a secure place to be. Enveloped by the dark and surrounded by stench, Jonah lifted his voice and praised God.

Praise is *giving glory to God in the midst of your circumstances.* It is not an option for a Christian; it is a command. The Bible says, "Sing to the LORD, who dwells in Zion; proclaim His deeds among the nations." (Psalm 9:11)

If lament is *inviting God into your sorrow,* then praise is the natural outcome. When you recognize God's presence, your reaction will be to focus on His glory, which will lead to praise. Even at the "roots of the mountains," in the acid bath of a fish's stomach, Jonah was able to praise the God he fled from, because in his sorrow he discovered God's presence.

Even in trials—especially in trials—Christians have reason to praise.

Lament, confession, celebration, and praise are small thing Christians intentionally do to open themselves to God's work of conforming them to the image of Christ. Instead of letting the tragedies of life break you, you can encounter God in your sorrow, pain, joy, and even sin. God is there in all of life's circumstances, ready to receive you when you press into Him.

Chapter 5: From isolation to connection

6.8 billion and counting. The world's population has never been greater; yet people struggle to find genuine friends. The popularity of blogs, e-mails, Facebook, and dating services reveals that people are desperate to connect with others. As with all of our needs, God provided the perfect plan. Only the church brings us together with our brothers and sisters in Christ to enjoy the fellowship God intended. But church isn't just a social network. Being part of the body of Christ means you can take off your mask and be real with other Christians. You'll find a depth of caring, love, sharing, and support that overflow from vibrant relationships with God. If you've never experienced that kind of fellowship with other believers, take this opportunity to move from isolation to connection by practicing these disciplines.

SPIRITUAL ISOLATION

There are a few things I'm good at and many things I'm bad at. Still other things I'm horrible at, among them the fact that I'm a terrible patient. Other than a couple of childhood illnesses, I hadn't been sick a day in my life until the first time a doctor diagnosed me with cancer. One surgery turned into three and a bonus stay in the hospital, where they used radiation to kill any remnant thyroid tissue left behind.

Of the four hospitalizations, the hardest one was the time I spent in the special room with lead walls after drinking radioactive iodine. Even though it didn't require coping with the effects of anesthesia and an incision, it was the worst.

It didn't start out well. During admission the nurse brought me the standard- issue hospital gown to wear. It didn't fit. "I need a larger size," I said. "This one is too small."

She looked at the label and replied, "This one is a large, and it's the biggest one we've got."

"Wait a minute," I said. "Isn't obesity a major medical problem?"

"Yes," she replied.

"Am I correct to assume that you have many patients who are my size or larger?"

"Yes," she said.

"Then why don't you have a gown that fits?"

This was a big deal to me because I hadn't brought anything with me except my street clothes. I had never dreamed the hospital wouldn't have something to fit me. Other hospitals had. Now I had nothing to wear.

Government regulations dictate that radiologists administer the exact dosage of radioactive iodine. The medicine arrived in the room. The doctor didn't. After about an hour I buzzed the front desk. "When will the doctor get here?" I asked.

The nurse called down to the radiology department. "He's busy right now, but he will be here when he can," she said.

For more than two hours, I waited with all my fears. *We scheduled the admittance into the hospital at his convenience, so where is he?* I thought. After waiting for what seemed a lifetime, he showed up. He was in the room for less than a minute as I sipped the radioactive iodine. He left, and the quarantine phase of my stay began.

Nurses brought food on disposable trays and set it by the door for me to retrieve after they left. I was like a caged animal. The only people allowed in the room were nurses, who came in to take my vitals. To avoid contamination, they had to wear protective gear and couldn't touch me.

I felt like a leper.

Early the next morning the safety officer checked me with his Geiger counter and said it was safe for me to leave the room. He said the head nurse would sign me out, and I'd be free to go. *Perfect,* I thought. *I can still make the 10:00 a.m. Bible study at church.* I called the church office and left a message to let the group know I would be there to teach. The class wouldn't start for three more hours, so I knew there would be no problem getting there on time, or so I thought. After an hour passed, I buzzed the desk. "The head nurse knows you are waiting, but she has a lot to do this morning," the kind voice on the other end of the intercom said. I continued to wait. When the head nurse didn't come, I buzzed the desk again. "She's still busy," the nurse said. "She's in an important meeting."

I looked at the clock and realized I needed to leave in 30 minutes to make it to the Bible study. "The safety officer has cleared me to leave," I said. "Please tell her that I'm a busy man too and that if she doesn't come down to discharge me within the next 30 minutes, I'm leaving without the discharge."

That's exactly what happened.

I know, I know. I acted like a jerk. I don't feel good about it. The best I can say in my defense is that the time I spent in isolation revealed how immature I really was. It's not just me either. Something happens to people when they are isolated.

Every now and then a television reporter puts a microphone into the face of a serial killer's neighbor and asks for a description of the criminal. Inevitably, the same term surfaces: "He was a loner," they say. "He kept to himself." The FBI described Eric Rudolph, the suspected bomber of Centennial Olympic Park in 1996, as a loner. Reporters used the same term to describe the convicted Unabomber, Ted Kaczynski, after they arrested him near Lincoln, Montana, in May 1996.

Although seasons of solitude are good for the soul (see chap. 3), long-term isolation isn't. God said, "It is not good that the man should be alone" (Gen. 2:18, KJV), so He created Eve as a wife for Adam. When Jesus sent His disciples on a mission trip, He sent them out in pairs (see Mark 6:7), and God designed His church to be a body of believers who share their lives and ministry together (see Acts 2:42-47). Yet many Christians find themselves in spiritual isolation. They minister alone, study alone, and

98

live their Christian lives alone. Though times of solitude are helpful to everyone, there is something unhealthy about being a Lone Ranger Christian. Think about it: even the Lone Ranger had Tonto.

CREATING CONNECTION

Sadly, loners aren't the only people suffering from spiritual isolation. It's possible to be alone in a crowd and not connect with anyone. This is most common in churches where self-disclosure is rare and excellence is valued more highly than authenticity. Brad Waggoner writes, "Less than a third of our churchgoers could confidently affirm they have high-quality relationships with fellow church members."[45] Too many church members are surrounded by people but have not connected with someone in a significant way. Waggoner states, "We must get past the idea of a 'friendly church' to the concept of a church of friends.'"[46] Everybody's church is friendly, but that doesn't mean people are forming significant relationships there.

Connection occurs through significant relationships, not through casual contact with acquaintances. Connection is forming relationships of mutual accountability and support with other believers. The starting point is to develop authentic relationships with other believers—to stop pretending that everything is fine when it isn't. Other helpful practices are to experience true Christian fellowship in community and to enter God's presence in corporate worship. Don't dismiss the importance of these practices just because you have friends, frequent fellowship events, and attend worship services. There is a difference between having friends and being real with them. There is also a difference between going to a fellowship at church and experiencing true Christian fellowship. And there is a vast difference between attending a worship service and entering God's presence in corporate worship.

The facade of spiritual perfection blocks genuine spiritual growth and destroys the capacity for intimacy with God and His people. On the other hand, authenticity facilitates both—something Pastor Ron learned by experience.

Ron had big dreams for his talented daughter, Tammy. When she was 12, she brought down the house at her church's talent show. She had sung several times as a child, but this was her first entry into adult singing. She left them stunned. Over the next four years she performed at several talent shows throughout the community and took home a blue ribbon every time. It was effortless. She was a natural. At one show more than a thousand people were in attendance. When Tammy sang, electricity filled the air. About a hundred kids ran down the aisle and screamed as though she were a rock star. The next year she auditioned for the television show "Star Search." Although she made the final cut, she didn't show up for the last call because her date that night was more important to her.

Tammy wasn't the brightest candle on the cake. Don't get me wrong. She was brilliant, but she lacked common sense. The final call for "Star Search" wasn't the only appointment she missed; Tammy had a hard time making it to school many mornings, resulting in truancy. Until 10:00 p.m. the night before graduation, it didn't appear that she would graduate, but at the final hour she turned in her missing assignments and graduated with her classmates.

At her graduation, Ron was shocked to see Tammy walk in with the valedictorian and the class president. He didn't know that the school administrators had asked her to sing the national anthem. As she approached the microphone to sing, the five thousand people in attendance went wild. Tears formed in Ron's eyes. He was proud of his little girl. He wasn't going to let everything else that was going on in her life rob him of this moment of pride. He relished it. He deserved it.

Tammy continued to show promise. Soon after graduation, she won a talent show at a local amusement park. "She's the most talented person we've heard in 12 years," the organizer of the event said. He then offered her a job singing and serving as an ambassador for the park. Tammy took the job, but management fired her a week later for coming to work late and neglecting her duties. That was fine with her; she got another job singing with a band from the area and started playing the local nightclub scene. That's when she started using marijuana. Soon she graduated to harder drugs.

Tammy married for the first time while she was four months pregnant. For the sake of the baby, Ron helped the new family establish themselves, providing a $10,000 down payment on a furnished mobile home. Soon her husband bailed, but she replaced him with a live-in boyfriend. Before long, she was pregnant again.

The drugs continued, and problems escalated. When Child Protective Services removed the children from the home due to neglect, Tammy's mother-in-law hired a lawyer and got custody of the children. Ron paid $2,500 to clean the trailer and another $1,500 to get out of the contract. Tammy had stripped its appliances— even the air conditioner—and sold them for drug money.

Tammy's third marriage ended like the other two, and she is now living with another man. "But the reality is that she is still our daughter and they are still our grandchildren," Ron says. Ron knows he and his wife did the best they could with all three of their girls. One of them is wayward. There's nothing they can do to change that, but they make sure they don't enable her behavior. "Our lives and commitment to God must continue," Ron says. "We cling to each other, and we cling to our faith."

Ron finds his church provides supportive relationships that help him cling to his faith. His friends and his church know about the situation with his daughter and are supportive of him. They provide him with a listening ear when he needs it and an opportunity to receive and give the grace of God. Ron doesn't let his problems force him into spiritual isolation. Instead, he turns to his friends at church, and they strengthen him. The truth is, without their help, Ron might not have survived the tragedy of a daughter who squandered her potential on drugs. With it, he finds the strength he needs in his faith and his faith community, and he experiences authentic worship with his church family.

Discretion is important with self disclosure, and church services can't become therapy sessions; but there is room for lament and sharing in church gatherings. The early church was diligent to support one another and to meet one another's needs. Only in such an environment, can broken people feel comfortable sharing their burdens and experience the healing love of God's family.

Acts 2:42-47 depicts the special type of fellowship that exists in the body of Christ. The Greek word *koinonia,* used in the New Testament, is translated *fellowship, partnership,* or *sharing. Koinonia* refers to the love relationship God has with His people, as well as the love relationship that believers are to share with others in the body of Christ. Sacrificial love, sharing, support, compassion, grace, unity, and service characterize *koinonia.* True fellowship is in the church when members' love for one another emanates from their love for the Head of the body, Jesus Christ. Churches can develop an atmosphere of *koinonia* if their members work together with God and one another to accomplish their mission and to become an authentic community of faith.

CREATING CONNECTION THROUGH WORSHP

Sometimes problems can be so heavy that they inhibit personal worship. In those times, believers can find their hope and express praise through the faith and optimism of their faith community. Instead of letting his family problems keep him from experiencing worship, Ron leaned into the strength of his church to carry him during his time of need. Robert Mulholland Jr. writes, "When we don't feel like worshiping, the community should carry us along in its worship. When we can't seem to pray, community prayer should enfold us. When the Scripture seems closed for us, the community should keep on reading, affirming and incarnating it around us."[47] Ron couldn't be "carried by his congregation" if he never allowed fellow believers to help him bear his burden.

In the previous chapter you read about the importance of lament in opening the door for authentic praise. The same is true with corporate worship. Church has to be a place where believers can be open and honest about their sorrows. Without authenticity, there can be no genuine worship experience. Kristine Suna-Koro writes, "Worship cannot be authentic and honest if an essential component such as lament is missing."[48] Ron's lament— *inviting God into his sorrow*—and his authenticity—*being his real self with other believers*—gave him the ability to experience God in worship.

When I was writing *Future Church*, something was stirring in me that I couldn't explain. It was a yearning, a longing for more. Analyzing worship experiences of churches across the country that were effective at reaching young adults was causing me to reflect on my own practice of worship. The sad truth is, I became better at analyzing worship than worshiping. One Friday afternoon I grabbed my laptop and made the following journal entry. I didn't intend to share it with anyone when I wrote it. It was my way of working out the angst I was feeling—a need to draw closer to God during worship and stop performing for the people I served. I reread it often; and every time I do, it still resonates with my desire to worship God in community.

Why Am I Standing Here?

I don't like being on stage where people look at me, evaluate me, judge me, ignore me, idealize me, minimize me, or put me in their box of who they think I am. I'd much rather sit on the back row, away from anyone's eyes or thoughts, where no one will notice if I weep or laugh, sing or sleep. I'd rather be in the corner, where it's safe.

Please don't get me wrong. I'm not complaining. Because there was a time when I couldn't be where I wanted to be, and it ripped the heart of my soul. The cancer didn't kill me, but not being able to do what I was chosen to do robbed my soul of its vitality. I was desperate to speak to you about Him; and when I couldn't, I felt incomplete. No, incomplete isn't the word. I felt worthless.

So today, I'm going to stand before you. Not because I'm better than you or smarter than you or wiser than you or more spiritual than you. I'm going to stand before you because I know this could be the week. This could be the week when we do more than have a worship service. It could be the week when we forget about me and we forget about you and we focus on Him and we truly worship.

But today I'm standing here, where I'd rather not be. In a few minutes, I'll stand before you and wrestle with every distraction to keep your attention on this message. I'm supposed to be thought-provoking yet lighthearted,

104

brilliant yet humble, thorough yet concise, timeless yet up-to-date.

And so I pray, "Let the fire fall, Lord! Bless us; drench us in Your grace! Descend on us with power! Let Your Spirit fill this place!"

I'm standing here because I don't know where else to stand. It is my destiny, my calling. But then again, this isn't about me; and it isn't about you, for that matter. It's about Him. So today I stand before you—no, make that beside you—before a holy God who is worthy of our worship and longs for us to come to church prepared to worship Him.

Could today be the day?

Even though I was standing in front of a crowd, I was experiencing isolation. My role made me feel more like a performer than a participant. I felt that people were judging me and evaluating the worship service instead of worshiping God. Whether they were or not isn't the point. That was the way I felt; and the truth is, that is what I was doing. I had become so analytical about worship that I had stopped worshiping. Today life is different. Although I still stand before a congregation and preach most Sundays, I am more alert to God and less conscious of them and their opinions of me.

The only thing that has changed is the attitude with which I enter the auditorium. During his remarks after the president nominated him to the United States Supreme Court, Judge Samuel Alito said, "The Supreme Court is an institution that I have long held in reverence." Later he commented, "I argued my first case before the Supreme Court in 1982, and I still vividly recall that day. I remember the sense of awe that I felt when I stepped up to the lectern."[49]

Alito holds the court in reverence. Standing at the lectern, he had a sense of awe. Those are the same feelings believers should experience when they stand before a holy God ready to bring Him praise, adoration, and worship.

When Isaiah beheld God's holiness (see Isaiah 6:1-8), he was devastated by the recognition of his sin. God then intervened to atone for Isaiah's sin, bringing him into a position of usefulness in the Lord's service. When believers worship, they catch a glimpse of God's glory, which results in repentance, spiritual transformation, and a desire for service. But for this to happen, believers must approach worship with reverence for and awe of God and with expectancy for their encounter with Him.

Creating Connection Through True Fellowship

Before the school bell stopped ringing, she slipped out of her seat, through the door, and into the hallway. Crystal didn't have to clear her desk. She had already put everything into her backpack, ready to start the weekend. Crystal was all about the weekend. In many ways, her weekend lasted most of the week.

Just a normal teenager, right? Not quite. At least she didn't think so. Crystal never felt normal. She felt more like an alien observing earthlings than a part of the human race. Normal is what she wanted but was never able to achieve. She always felt different. As far as she was concerned, everyone else was normal; they had nice, predictable lives. She was the odd girl out. It wasn't that she wasn't popular. She was very popular, particularly with the boys. As she entered the opaque world between childhood and seductress, the boys paid her plenty of attention.

With time Crystal's skirts got shorter, and her morals got lower. She loved the way boys looked at her and the way men stared at her. After a while, flirting wasn't enough. She needed more. It wasn't just the confusing emotions that rushed through her young body; it was her need to feel normal. To feel accepted. To feel anything.

When it happened, it felt great. When it was over, Crystal felt empty. She wanted more. She got less. One by one, she pleasured herself with every boy or man she wanted. It became a numbers game—how many men she could sleep with before she was legal. Sex became as common to Crystal as brushing her teeth or combing her hair. Before she turned 18, she had slept with men three times her age and had wrecked several marriages, but she never got what she craved. One encounter led to another, and every encounter led nowhere. She was empty, longing for more.

She yearned for stability and direction.

Crystal's dad was an executive working for big stakes on foreign oil fields. The money was good, but it wasn't the best environment for raising a family. Before her 18th birthday, Crystal had lived in a dozen countries, most of them in the Middle East. The variety stimulated her mind; she attended the best schools with the best teachers and was always at the top of her class. Schoolwork came easy for her. What didn't come easy for her were meaningful relationships. Her parents gave her no spiritual guidance, except to tell her to experience everything and make up her own mind what she wanted to believe. That is what they said; but deep down inside, Crystal knew they didn't want her to believe what her grandmother did.

When Crystal was 10, she spent the summer at her grandmother's house in rural Kentucky. This was the only time in her life that she felt normal. Her grandmother gave her chores around the house and allowed her to help cook dinner and wash dishes. One morning her grandma took

Crystal by the hand and walked with her from the farm across a creek, over a bridge, and down the road to church. It wasn't just any church. It was a church her grandfather had built with his own hands and her grandma had poured hours of work into. Along the way, her grandma showed Crystal places of significance to the family and told one family story after another. For the first time in her life, Crystal felt connected. When they arrived at the church— her family's church—she joined the other boys and girls for Vacation Bible School. She memorized the Bible verses, listened to the mission stories, and played with the other kids. It was the happiest time in her life.

Now happiness eluded Crystal. She chased it down, grabbed it, but was never able to hold on to it; it always slipped through her fingers. She didn't regain the stability she felt that summer in Kentucky until she was 19 and met Hank. Hank was different from the other boys. He was a perfect gentleman with her, never taking advantage of her advances. In a way, it was frustrating, but in another way, it was comforting. Hank liked Crystal but not for the reasons boys had always liked her. He saw something in her that she didn't even see in herself. He saw a person of value. Crystal did something she had never done before: she made Hank her exclusive boyfriend. All was well. Then it happened.

A couple of weeks after she and Hank hooked up, Crystal was hanging out with some friends at the mall when an old boyfriend offered to give her a ride home. But he didn't take her home. He pulled behind a warehouse and turned off the engine. Crystal recognized the look in his eyes and tried to explain that she was different now; she wasn't interested in making out with him. But he wouldn't listen and started unbuttoning her blouse. She struggled and said, "No, I don't want to do this." Her refusal seemed to turn him on more. They struggled. He won. Crystal stopped moving, going limp as he raped her. When he was done, she got out of the car and walked home.

Why couldn't she have what other girls have? Why couldn't she have normality in her life? Why did she have to put up with creeps like this? Crystal thought. She wanted a clean break from the past. She wanted some kind of status with Hank that other boys would respect, so she convinced him to let her move in with him. That decision was easy for her, a no-brainer. The next decision she would have to make wouldn't be so easy. Crystal was about to face the most difficult decision of her life.

Sometimes Crystal had missed her period because of intense physical activity, so she didn't think anything about it for the first few months. But when the fourth month rolled around, she got concerned and went to the doctor. Sure enough, she was pregnant. Because the rape happened about the same time she and Hank first slept together, she wasn't sure who the father was. She was afraid to talk to Hank about it, but she knew she had to. The guilt was gnawing at her soul. She had messed up her own life for good, but she had no right to ruin Hank's life too.

For perhaps the first time in her life, Crystal was thinking about someone else's happiness and not just her own. She didn't quite know how to start the conversation, so she just jumped in. "Hank, I'm pregnant." Hank didn't say a word. She continued. "I don't know if you're the father or not." Hank remained quiet. "A couple weeks after we hooked up, an old boyfriend raped me. He could be the father. I don't know." Hank moved over to Crystal, held her tight, and said, "I'm sorry, Baby. I'm sorry."

She melted into his arms and cried.

They talked about it and decided not to keep the baby. What was best for everybody concerned was for her to terminate the pregnancy. Crystal already had a follow-up appointment with the doctor, so she decided to wait until then to talk to him about the procedure. The next time Crystal went to the doctor, he showed her the sonogram. She saw her baby—not a fetus—sucking her little thumb. Crystal couldn't go through with it. For the first time in her life, she wanted to make an unselfish decision. In her desperation she turned to her parents, who, of course, told her to get the abortion. She had no one else to turn to. No one except her grandmother's God. She hadn't prayed since she was 10 years old attending Vacation Bible School at her grandparents' Kentucky church. Around eight that night she started praying. She prayed for wisdom and courage to do the right thing. "Jesus, save me from myself. I'm sorry. Please heal all the wrongs I've done and the people I've hurt. I've heard You can do miracles. I need one now. Help me know what to do. Help me do what's right. Amen."

Crystal went to sleep and slept securely in her Heavenly Father's arms. The next day her dad called and asked her, "So what are you going to name the baby?" She couldn't believe it. Not in a million years did she expect to get support from her dad.

She had written Hank a note telling him she was going to keep the baby; but if he wanted, she would go away, and he would never have to hear from her again. When Hank found the note, he found Crystal and said, "You've stolen my thunder."

"What do you mean?" Crystal asked.

"I was moving some boxes in the back room at work when it hit me that we have to keep the baby."

"When did that happen?" she asked.

He replied, "Oh, I think it was about eight o'clock. So you want to get married or what?" Hank asked. Crystal passed on the "or what" but took him up on the "get married" part of the proposal.

Hank and Crystal had some rough years; but they built a life together, and Crystal found the happiness that had eluded her for so long. One Sunday morning she was sitting in church next to her husband, who was now a deacon, and watched as two of her teenage children lead in worship. Later in the service another of her children escorted the kids out of the auditorium for children's church, and her youngest child lit an altar candle.

In that moment Crystal was transported to a country church in Kentucky—a church her grandfather built with his own hands. A church where she learned how to pray— where her grandmother taught her that she was connected and that she was loved.

The church where she first sang the words

Amazing grace! how sweet the sound That saved a wretch like me!
I once was lost, but now am found,
Was blind, but now I see.

Crystal wiped away the tear that was forming in her eyes, smiled, and joined her congregation as they sang the final verse of that hymn:

When we've been there ten thousand years,
Bright shinning as the sun,
We've no less days to sing God's praise Than when we first begun.[50]

Just a brief encounter with God's presence in a small Kentucky church had a lifelong impact on Crystal. It became her North Star, the only sense of stability she had. Now she and her husband are providing for her children what she didn't have as a child, and Crystal is living a transformed life because of her encounter with Jesus. One community of believers changed the trajectory of Crystal's life—and her children's. The leaders of the Vacation Bible School Crystal attended never knew their impact on Crystal's life. Yet the members of that rural-Kentucky church are bearing exponential fruit for the Kingdom because they were faithful to connect Crystal to God and His body, the church.

I love the church, and I get defensive when people criticize it. A few years ago Leadership Network asked me to analyze George Barna's book *Revolution* and to develop an interactive survey[51] to learn whether the readers of their publication *The Advance were* seeing the same trends Barna had identified. One theme of the book was that relating to a local church and/or attending a worship service is optional for a follower of Christ and, further, is likely to be detrimental to spiritual development. According to Barna, involvement in a local church makes one less likely to be "Spirit-led, faith-focused, scripturally literate and biblically obedient."[52] Barna gives no basis for his conclusions in the book. He does not buttress them with research; he just states them. Worse than the poor scholarship, his statements are counter to the teaching of Scripture.

The New Testament pattern was daily worship (see Acts 2:46), and the writer of Hebrews encouraged regular church attendance (see Heb. 10:24-25). No doubt the church can improve what it does, but it is still the bride of Christ. Improve it if it is lacking, but abandoning it won't benefit any believer.

The church isn't perfect, because it is composed of imperfect people. Although the church will never achieve perfection this side of heaven, it can strive for authenticity and unity. Breaking out of spiritual isolation and living life with an authentic community of believers are small things believers can intentionally do to open themselves to God's work of conforming them to the image of Christ. Notice that I wrote "authentic" community, not "perfect" community.

Paul was brutal with the Corinthian church in 1 Corinthians 3:1-9, calling them spiritual babies. He wrote this because they were a divided church, unable to work together. Some people were attaching themselves to Paul and others to Apollos. They had rivalries; they weren't unified. Something had to change. Have you ever had a church relationship like that? I have. I've served a church where people couldn't agree on anything except that they didn't like one another. Of course, I blamed them, and they blamed me; but the truth is, we both were right. Barna may have a point if he was referring to a church like the one I'm remembering or the Corinthian church that Paul wrote about. But Paul didn't give up on them.

Paul encouraged the believers to focus on unity. He wrote, "We are God's co-workers. You are God's field, God's building" (1 Cor. 3:9). His point was that there was a variety of different roles in Kingdom work, but every church member's work was equally important. The important thing was that they work together to build on the foundation laid by Jesus (see 1 Cor. 3:11).

Paul had a similar message for the church in Philippi: "If then there is any encouragement in Christ, if any consolation of love, if any fellowship with the Spirit, if any affection and mercy, fulfill my joy by thinking the same way, having the same love, sharing the same feelings, focusing on one goal. Do nothing out of rivalry or conceit, but in humility consider others as more important than yourselves. Everyone should look out not only for his own interests, but also for the interests of others" (Phil. 2:1-4). The believers shared a common fellowship with the Holy

Spirit. This unity gave them a common life together—a life of fellowship with one another—and a common purpose—to live in love, humility, and service to one another in the body of Christ.

A few years ago we had an open-mike night at Hemet Valley Baptist Church during a Sunday evening service for members to respond to these questions: What are your fondest memories of our church? When were we at our very best? About 15 people spoke, each of them with a different story; but really, all of the stories made the same point: our church is at its best when the members are working together to accomplish something. Our members said not only that the church was at its best then but also that those times were significant springboards for spiritual growth.

As I look into my rearview mirror, my greatest memories of church life are times when a unified church worked toward a common goal. When I was a child, our small church in Edmonson, Texas, had a revival. I don't mean a revival meeting; I mean a revival. The leaders extended the meeting over several weeks because of the overwhelming response.

So many people accepted Christ that during the final service, all we did was baptize new converts. Though I was only in grade school, I actively shared my faith with my friends, and some of them came to faith in Christ through those efforts. In some ways the fires of that revival meeting are still burning, because that was the first time I heard God speak to me about becoming a pastor. I remember that the movement of the Spirit was amazing, but I also remember that we were doing this together. Everyone was participating in God's work of drawing people to Himself and to a loving community of faith.

Berkeley Avenue Baptist Church in Turlock, California, had an annual Memorial Day weekend campout when I was their pastor. One year more than two hundred of us spent the weekend together and enjoyed a time of rich fellowship. The baptism we had in the river is among my fondest memories of my time at that church. I've got similar stories to tell with every church where I've been a pastor or a member. I'll never forget the mission trip that First Baptist Church of Alameda, New Mexico, took to remodel a 150-year-old building built by slaves in Lake Village, Arkansas; or the migrant mission project that Lighthouse Baptist Church in Seaside, California, conducted, giving clothes to less fortunate people and presenting the gospel to them; or the sense of unity and purpose the members of First Baptist Church of Palm Desert, California, felt as we built our new auditorium with our own hands.

It wasn't just that we were doing something to change the world in these churches. It's that we were doing it together, enjoying Christian fellowship as we grew in our relationship with one another and God. Glenn McDonald writes, "A spiritually vital congregation has to affirm, 'We get together to build each other up, and the Kingdom is built as a consequence.'"[53] True fellowship rarely happens over a cup of coffee or a plate of spaghetti. Real fellowship happens beside a hospital bed, over a paint can, or in a committee meeting. Whenever we underscore the together in working together, we come to understand what it means to live in an authentic community. Christians develop relationships with God and His people when they work together for the cause of Christ, resulting in Kingdom expansion and personal spiritual growth.

Every Bible-believing church provides a unique opportunity for believers to connect with God through worship and with others through authentic relationships and true fellowship. These important disciplines of the faith are small things Christians intentionally do to open themselves to God's work of conforming them to the image of Christ.

CHAPTER 6: FROM ENTITLEMENT TO MINISTRY

If I'm not careful, I can begin to think the world revolves around me. When I walk into a restaurant, the waiter brings me whatever I ask for, in class my students conform to my wishes, and at the office our staff is always eager to help. It's not just me either. I've noticed other Christians who have developed a sense of entitlement. They come to church and want things their way. If they don't get it, they move on to another church that will cater to their needs. A gravitational force surrounds people that make them believe they are the main actors in life and everyone else, including God, is the supporting cast. That force is not from God. God's calling is for us to be servants, not to be served. Discover these strategic disciplines for joining God's work of ministry and for serving others in Jesus' name.

CRITICAL NEEDS

It was hot, sticky, and miserable. The shade did not provide any respite in the outdoor sauna. It only made it harder to see. Wearing coveralls and a white hat with a huge bill, Gayle withstood the one-hundred-degree temperature and 100 percent humidity to pass out Bibles to underprivileged children in Arkansas. By all accounts, she shouldn't be there. Just a few summers before, she had suffered a heatstroke and seizures while vacationing in Chiapas, Mexico. She still suffers ill effects from that trip today. Regardless, she was there because she wanted to be part of her church's mission trip; she wanted to do something good for someone else. Little did she know that the trip would have such an impact on her and her husband.

While attending Jericho Week in Glorieta, New Mexico, in July 1997, Bekah heard about the needs of the impoverished people living along the Mississippi Delta. Burdened, she asked her church, First Baptist Church of Beverly Hills, to purchase the North American Mission Board video that depicts their struggle, *A River Runs Through It,* and move the annual home-missions study from spring 1998 to fall 1997. With church approval she decorated the fellowship hall to look like the banks of the mighty river and prepared a meal of beans and rice. Unlike sponsors of the one- thousand-dollar-a-plate meals for politicians, Bekah wasn't trying to raise money; she was trying to raise awareness.

After participants ate the modest meal and watched the video, their consensus was "We need to do something to help but what?" Ray and Susan, who were visiting the church, suggested they come to their community, Lake Village, Arkansas, on a mission trip. Though the film producers did not feature it in the video, it is along the Mississippi Delta and knows poverty's blight. The group decided their pastor should study the situation and recommend an appropriate course of action at a future meeting.

With poverty's images etched on his heart, Pastor Tom prayed for direction.

One sentence from the video stuck in his mind: "Children who wear nice school clothes outperform those with tattered clothes." After flying to Lake Village, he asked the church to earmark $10,000 to purchase one pair of shoes and one set of clothes for every child living beneath the poverty line.

Lake Village has its share of poverty. The average per capita income in Chicot County is 50 percent of the national average. As many as 59 percent of the children, according to the U.S. Census Bureau, live in poverty. Joyce Vaught, the superintendent of schools, says 85 percent of the children in her school district qualify for the government's free-lunch program.

Compared with the glaring need, $10,000 isn't much; but it is exorbitant to First Baptist Church of Beverly Hills, a church running 55 in worship. After all, with only 20 persons attending the missions banquet, it represented about $500 a plate—not bad for beans and rice. The church approved the plan, but God had something bigger in mind— much bigger.

AN EXPLODING MINISTRY

In June Pastor Tom flew to Lake Village again to meet with religious and civic leaders in the community. Ninety minutes into the meeting, the group finished organizing seven committees and securing a promise of cooperation from everyone at the table. The excitement was building, and so was the size of the project. Members of the church

119

gave, not $10,000 but $15,000. One member began to tell his business associates about the mission's project, and they gave an additional $60,000.

With $75,000 in hand, the pastor began calling clothing manufacturers to learn whether he could purchase the clothing direct from the factories at a savings. The extra effort paid off. With the money they raised, he purchased merchandise with a retail value of $250,000. Instead of giving some children one set of clothes and one pair of shoes, they expanded the project to give all 583 elementary children a complete school wardrobe, some church clothes, and a New Testament.

Not wanting to spend any of the $75,000 on transportation and incidentals, each member had to pay $500 to go on the mission trip. Gayle was the first member to sign up. To her delight, her husband, Brian, a member of Los Angeles's Jewish community, wanted to go too. Though Gayle was active in the church, Brian was not a Christian and rarely attended. Occasionally, he accompanied Gayle to work days at the church but only so that she could complete her assignment more quickly. This time something was different. After signing up, he said, "I'm 61 years old, and I've never done anything good for anybody. This gives me a chance to change that."

Thursday, August 20, 1998, Gayle and Brian and the others on their mission team caught a flight to Little Rock, Arkansas, knowing they were in the center of God's will, ready to touch the lives of strangers. After touching down, they transferred to a church bus for a $2^1/_2$-hour ride to Lake Village. They arrived around 8:30 p.m., and a police escort directed them through town to Lake Village Baptist Church. That evening they enjoyed a southern-fried catfish dinner, prepared by the Chamber of Commerce, and went to their host homes to get some rest. In about 36 hours

120

1,800 people would inundate them. They needed all the sleep they could get.

The task was overwhelming. Preparing for the block party and distributing more than 15,000 items within a couple of hours demanded cooperation from everyone. Government and civic agencies joined the religious community in planning and implementing the block party. Overnight what looked like an outdoor flea market sprang up on the empty lot east of New Hope Baptist Church. Five funeral-home tents flanked the 80-by-12-foot National Guard tent to provide shade for the people who would besiege them the next day to receive school uniforms for their children. Workers unfolded 80 tables they had borrowed from surrounding churches and set them up under the tents.

Earlier in the month, several trucks had delivered the merchandise to a nearby office building. Collectively, it would have taken a standard-sized moving truck to transport everything at the same time. Now the workers had to haul all of the boxes to the church, carry them to the proper location, and display their contents for distribution. Friday was exhausting; but as the sun set over Lake Chicot, the members of the mission team were anxious for the next day.

The next morning in the blistering heat, the mission team arrived at the block party to begin its ministry. The crowds deluged them. Gayle passed out Bibles at the first table. As she handed a Bible to each child, she said, "Here, I want you to have this Bible; it is from First Baptist Church of Beverly Hills, and it is just for you." Her husband, Brian, escorted the families through the maze to get them to the right place in the correct order. As Brian helped a man take his children through the line, the man gazed straight at the ground and wouldn't look Brian in the eye. When they were done, the man looked up and said, "God bless you all for helping us. I don't know how we could have gotten clothes for the kids without your help."

"No," Brian said. "God bless you and your children."

Following the block party, some members of the mission team and the community went to Cricket's, a local restaurant for lunch. With the spiritual adrenaline still pumping, someone began to sing a hymn; and everyone else, even the other customers, joined in. It was a revival meeting on Main Street. The owner of Cricket's fell under the Holy Spirit's conviction when the mission team was in her restaurant. She and her daughter opened their entire inventory of beer and poured a thousand dollars down the drain. Cricket closed the sports bar in the back room and opened the doors to a local pastor to start a church in the restaurant.

"When the mission team was here," Cricket said, "I learned that God can be in the public without hurting your business." Now the first thing a customer sees when they walk into Cricket's is a 15-foot mural of the Last Supper.

UNEXPECTED BLESSINGS

Following the joint worship service Sunday morning, five pastors donned baptismal garb and walked into Lake Chicot—four black pastors, along with Gayle's pastor, Pastor Tom. While the choir sang an old spiritual, Brian, Gayle's husband, walked into the water. Yes, Gayle's husband had accepted Christ.

This was the culmination of a long journey for Brian. One Sunday morning in April 1998, he had driven his wife to church in his newly restored 1961 Corvette. The pastor, a car buff himself, wanted a closer look when he saw the car. A three-hundred-horsepower 350 CID Chevy V8 under the hood and a Borg Warner four-speed, close-ratio manual transmission attached to the drive train made the car irresistible. "Can you give me a ride around the block?" the pastor asked. Brian gladly took him for a spin.

When they arrived back at the church, the pastor had another request: "Why don't you come on up for my class on basic Baptist principles? I'd love to have you in the group."

Brian excused himself. "I haven't shaved in three days, and I plan on detailing the car this morning." The pastor wouldn't take no for an answer, so Brian acquiesced. Brian describes the class as the turning point for him. After it was over, he started attending worship on a regular basis. During the invitation, he felt twinges of guilt and urges to go forward and talk to the pastor, but he resisted.

Little by little, however, Brian was getting involved in the life of the church. He agreed to go on the mission trip with his wife and to be the webmaster of the church's Web site. A couple of weeks prior to the mission trip, he met with the pastor to discuss the Web site, but the pastor had another agenda: "Have you given any consideration to becoming a Christian? If so, I could baptize you in Lake Chicot on the mission trip." Under the conviction of the Holy Spirit, Brian prayed to receive Christ.

Gayle watched from the amphitheater as Brian walked into the water. "In the name of the Father and the Son and the Holy Spirit, I baptize you, my brother..." She had signed up for a mission trip to help others and found that she received more than she gave. She couldn't have asked for a greater gift than seeing Brian be baptized. On the mission trip she and her husband were ministers, touching the lives of others from the overflow of God's blessing.

JOINING GOD'S WORK OF MINISTRY

Ministry *is participating with God and cooperating with His people to serve His purposes.* Ministry isn't just for clergy. It is for ordinary people too -people like Gayle and Brian. For too long the church has reserved "real" ministry for the clergy and relegated the laity to helping or watching roles. This couldn't be further from the New Testament concept of ministry. First Peter 2:9 calls the people of God "a holy priesthood." The verse is not just referring to those on the church's payroll; it describes all believers. From the biblical perspective, ministry isn't something the church pays professionals to do; it is every believer's opportunity and obligation. Ministry is for every believer. Think about the disciples. They weren't religious professionals; they were ordinary people like Gayle and Brian. Yet God used them to change the world.

Ministry Is Participating with GOD

On the mission trip Gayle, Brian, and the other members of their group discovered that they were part of something much bigger than they could have dreamed up and pulled off. This was God-sized work, and God had invited them to join His work.

In 1 Thessalonians 3:2 Paul called Timothy "God's co-worker" and said in 1 Corinthians 3:9 that we are "God's co-workers." In Acts 21:19 Paul acknowledged that his success among the Gentiles was because God was working through him. Ministry isn't something believers do for God; we do it *with* Him. We participate with God in His work. The mission team learned that God could use their simple acts of kindness to do something significant—like start a new church in Cricket's Restaurant and help the community take steps toward racial reconciliation.

124

After baptizing Brian and two others from his church, Pastor Tom asked one of the pastors where he should stand as they baptized their candidates. "No, you don't understand," the pastor said. "We've talked about it among ourselves, and you're baptizing our people too." The fact that they were having an interracial worship service was groundbreaking; that a white man would baptize black persons in this region of the country was scandalous. In Lake Village the dentist's office has two doors—the front door for "whites" and a side door for "coloreds." Townspeople refer to New Hope Baptist Church as the black church and Lake Village Baptist Church as the white church. They are segregated.

This mission trip was different. Mayor Bush said, "Blacks and whites, rich and poor worked together." Distributing more than 15,000 items within a couple of hours demanded cooperation from everyone. It extended beyond the racial divide. Government and civic agencies joined the religious community in planning and implementing the block party. The joint worship service chipped away at the cultural racism and encouraged Christian unity among the races. Jeraldine, a choir member at New Hope Baptist Church, summed up its impact: "We shop together, we work together, and we eat together; but we don't worship together—that is, until the mission trip." Working together led to worshiping together and had now led to observing together one of the sacred ordinances of the church. A lifelong resident of Lake Village, 94-year-old Idell Karal Smith said, "This was the first time I ever saw blacks and whites baptized together." She continued, "Times have changed, and people have changed too." Though Reverend Haney, the pastor of New Hope, doesn't believe this one event reversed all the racism of the past, with a sly smile he said, "It's a start."

Ministry is much more than a human endeavor. It involves participating with God. Gayle and Brian and their colleagues were not doing relief work; they were doing God's work, and they weren't doing it alone. God was with them, and they were participating with Him.

Ministry Is Cooperating with God's People

Christians don't minister in isolation. They do it in cooperation with God's people. This doesn't mean believers can't be alone when they minister, just that they do the ministry with a cooperative spirit, in the name of the Lord, and as representatives of the body of Christ. Pastor Tom served as a catalyst for bringing God's people together to work in cooperation with one another. He involved members of his church with the members of the churches of Lake Village.

Ministry involvement can extend beyond the Christian community. Remember that Brian wasn't a Christian when the pastor enlisted him to help. Also, the Beverly Hills business community donated $60,000 toward the goal, and local government agencies cooperated with the effort. Often great ideas don't get off the ground because of turfism. If people are busy protecting their turf, they lose the opportunity to cooperate with others and to participate with God in what He is doing. The body of Christ is not to function this way.

As believers grow in Christ and do the work of ministry, one result is unity in the body of Christ. They can learn to work together, putting aside their differences to accomplish God's will. This can happen only if they are participating with God. If believers submit to God's agenda and put His kingdom first (see Matt. 6:33), they can cooperate with one another in ministry. Paul taught pastors

126

to cooperate with God's people, equipping them for the work of the ministry (see Eph. 4:12).

JOINING GOD'S WORK OF MINISTRY THROUGH SERVICE

At the heart of ministry is service. Service is *ministering in Jesus' name and with His love to meet others' needs, fulfill our calling, and bring glory to God.* [54] The Greek word for *ministry, diakonia,* denotes waiting a table. In a general sense it means a 'discharge of service' in genuine love."[55] No doubt, those involved in this mission trip were serving others. It was all about service. They served the children and their families; but in a broader sense they also served the school district, the local churches, and the community at large. According to the New Testament, ministers serve believers, nonbelievers, and even God.

SERVICE MEETS NEEDS

The driving force behind this mission trip was the plight of the children along the Mississippi Delta. Pastor Tom and the church wanted to do something to help those children. Those ministering gave the children more than shoes; they gave them dignity. Service typically begins with a nagging need and a desire to meet the need. The desire becomes a driving passion, an unquenchable compulsion to help someone.

As a storm brewed offshore, Ed called his family to discover their plans for evacuation. He had grown up in Kenner, just outside New Orleans, and most of his family still lived in the area. Ed tried to persuade his dad to leave, but he was adamant and wouldn't budge. He wanted to ride out the storm. Ed's grandmother and uncle planned to weather the storm at his business establishment downtown. His sister and her fiancé decided to go to Tennessee, and his mother was going to Shreveport. His cousin was in East Jefferson General Hospital in Metairie, and Ed assumed he would stay there.

Ed wasn't too worried when the storm hit. Though he wasn't happy that his father was being so stubborn, he figured he could take care of himself. Besides, Ed wasn't a worrying sort of fellow. His training as a naval officer prepared him to assess a situation and then take appropriate and measured action. He had done just that.

He knew everyone's plans, and he had survived a few storms himself. It wasn't that he was complacent—far from it. It was that he had done what he could do, so why worry about the rest? However, Hurricane Katrina wasn't just any storm. When the levees broke, everything changed.

Without delay Ed called his dad. No answer. *Was he OK and the phone service just out, or was he in trouble?* Ed didn't know. His resolve not to worry began to weaken.

He went through his personal phone book, calling everyone. No one answered. Ed was more than concerned now; he was getting nervous. Landlines were out, cell-phone towers inoperable. Even though some of his family had left the area, their cell phones weren't working because they had New Orleans area codes. From the news reports, Ed knew that a levee had broken near his uncle's business and that the water was rising in the area where his father lived. Even if the water hadn't breached his house, Ed knew there were no electrical and water services. In particular, he was concerned for his father's health. Diabetics can't survive long without food or medicine.

For several days, Ed was in the dark. The only news he had was from the television. By profession Ed is an engineer; in fact, he works as the chief engineer aboard his ship. He lives under stressful conditions every day of his life. If he messes up, the ship stops moving. He is calm, calculated, and always under control. *Control*—now that's a good word to describe him but not in a bad sense; he's not a control freak, but he's always in control of himself and tries to control his circumstances. During Katrina he felt out of control. He couldn't handle it. He was willing to do anything, but all he could do was pray. And he did. Ed interceded for his family with intensity.

Ministry grows from a need. The need becomes so compelling that other priorities tumble, and all attention goes to participating with God and cooperating with His people in serving others to meet their needs. In Acts 6, it was the ministry of meeting the widows' physical needs. For Ed it was the ministry of prayer, interceding for those in need. On the mission trip, it was the ministry of providing clothing and dignity to underprivileged schoolchildren. In all of these cases, believers were serving others to meet their needs.

A couple days after Katrina, Ed reconnected with his family. Almost everyone was OK. He knew his mom and sister were OK, because they had evacuated. As it turned out, his father had reconsidered and fled to Lake Charles, Louisiana, taking refuge in a church that provided him with the necessities and the medicine he needed. Only the Lord knows if this change of mind was a direct result of Ed's prayers. Regardless, his father's escape was nothing short of miraculous. Without water or electricity, he needed to get out; but the floodwaters were so high that he couldn't. When the city got the pumps working, the floodwaters receded enough that he was able to drive to the interstate.

Ed knew these family members were OK, but he still hadn't heard about his grandmother, uncle, and cousin. For two weeks he waited and heard nothing, so he continued to pray. God answered his prayers. His grandmother and uncle hadn't gone downtown near where a levee broke, as they had planned. Instead, they had headed north and avoided the storm. Ed's cousin, however, didn't make it. Officials had transported him from the hospital in Louisiana to Houston, where he died. "I went home in December,' Ed says, "The damage to the city was terrible." While he was home, he went to church with his dad and watched his sister and her fiancé get married. "What began as a time of great anxiety and frustration turned to calm and peace," Ed says. That happens when people minister by praying.

Everybody's ultimate need is for salvation through Jesus Christ. True Christian service always makes the connection between the act of service and the motivation behind that service—the love of Christ. As you perform acts of kindness, pray and look for ways to connect your service to the gospel.

SERVICE FULFILLS OUR CALLING

In 2007, while on stateside assignment from her mission field, Dara returned to the International Learning Center in Rockville, Virginia, and looked at the Cloud of Witnesses board, a plaque that contains the names of Southern Baptist missionaries who gave their lives in the call of duty. This time she was looking for a specific name— Karen Watson. In 2003 Dara was in the same room with Watson—this very room—as they wrote their letters that no one would open except in the event of their deaths.[56]

As a part of missionaries' training, instructors challenge new appointees to count the cost of Christian service and to realize that some of them might pay the ultimate sacrifice. Dara and Watson wrote their letters at the same time, sitting next to each other. No one except Dara knows what her own letter says. That isn't true of Watson. Fulfilling her calling meant laying down her life.

130

When Watson heard God's call to go to Iraq, she responded by resigning from her job and by selling her car, house, and other possessions. When she left, everything she owned was contained in a duffel bag. Today that bag is a reminder of the work she did in telling people in Iraq about Jesus Christ. Watson's family shared her story with the president of the Southern Baptist International Mission Board, Jerry Rankin, at her funeral. Rankin then took Watson's message of sacrifice to a mission conference in New Orleans. He encouraged students, faculty, and staff at New Orleans Baptist Theological Seminary to consider missions, not from an obligation to fulfill the Great Commission but because they were compelled by the love of Jesus.

Rankin said, "Media and culture—they just don't get it. Why would anyone go to a place that their lives would be at risk?" He added, "We have all succumbed to a culture and a philosophy where it is all about us, it's all about our comfort, all about our security, all about our future in this life. They never understand that there is something worth giving your life to. There is a purpose that's worth dying for. But the world doesn't understand that." Rankin said no one becomes obedient to the point of giving his or her life through a sense of obligation because Jesus said to go. He said, "No, you are driven by a passion in your heart for a lost world."[57]

Watson left only one other thing behind—the letter she wrote at the International Learning Center. It says:

Dear Pastor Phil and Pastor Roger,

You should be opening this letter only in the event of death.

When God calls, there are no regrets. I tried to share my heart with you as much as possible, my heart for the Nations. I wasn't called to a place. I was called to Him. To obey was my objective; to suffer was expected. His glory was my reward; His glory is my reward.

One of the most important things to remember right now is to preserve the work.... I am writing this as if I am still working among my people group.

I thank you all so much for your prayers and support. Surely your reward in Heaven will be great. Thank you for investing in my life and spiritual well-being. Keep sending missionaries out. Keep raising up fine young pastors.

In regards to any service, keep it small and simple. Yes, simple; just preach the gospel. If Jason Buss or his dad is available, have them sing a pretty song. Be bold and preach the life saving, life changing, forever eternal GOSPEL. Give glory and honor to our Father.

The Missionary Heart:

Care more than some think is wise.

Risk more than some think is safe.

Dream more than some think is practical.

Expect more than some think is possible.

I was called not to comfort or success but to obedience.

Some of my favorite Scriptures are: Isaiah 6—you know the one; 2 Corinthians 5:15-21; 1 Peter 1:3; Colossians 4:2-6; Romans

15:20; Psalms 25 and 27. You can look
through my Scofield and see where it is
marked. Please use only what you want or
feel is best.

There is no joy outside of knowing Jesus
and serving Him. I love you two and my
church family.

In His care,

Salaam, Karen[58]

Dara commented on her colleague's sacrifice by
saying, "Karen lived through bomb threats; kidnapping
threats; power outages; and being a single, white female in
a male-dominated Muslim world. These were the conflicts
in her life, and in the end she lived out Philippians 1:21,
"For me, living is Christ and dying is gain."[59]

Watson fulfilled her calling with her life and in her
death. Her testimony continues to inspire others to live out
their callings, even if it means sacrificing. Some people
fulfill their callings by selling everything and moving to
Iraq, others by joining their churches on a mission trip. Still
others do something in their own communities.

SERVICE BRINGS GLORY TO GOD

As important as meeting needs and fulfilling our calling
are, bringing glory to God is the ultimate reason Christians
minister. In her letter Watson wrote, "His glory was my
reward; His glory is my reward." Why did she write the
same phrase twice? Certainly to underscore that while she
was on earth, her reward was God's glory; and now that she
is in heaven, the same is true. I'm confident that she meant
every word she wrote in that letter, but make no mistake
about it—her ultimate goal was to bring glory to her God.

Glory is "weighty importance and shining majesty that accompany God's presence."[60] When we give weight to or honor God, we are not conferring glory on Him but recognizing the glory that is part of His nature. When we praise and give glory to God, we are acknowledging who He is, His majesty, and His importance (see Pss. 22:23; 86:12).

We bring glory to God when we give to Him the praise and worship He is due.

We seek to align our will with His and to serve Him. Instead of choosing our own way and advancing our own reputation, we try to exalt God in all things. Paul wrote, "Through the proof of this service, they will glorify God for your obedience to the confession of the gospel of Christ, and for your generosity in sharing with them and with others" (2 Cor. 9:13). We bring glory to God when we serve others in the name of Jesus, lifting up the truth of His salvation.

When you join God's work of ministry by serving others, you are able to meet their needs, fulfill your calling, and bring glory to God.

JOINING GOD'S WORK OF MINISTRY THROUGH SACRIFICE

Sometimes ministering to others and glorifying God require sacrifice. Stephen was a respected leader in the Jerusalem church who proclaimed the truth of Jesus Christ. In Acts 7:1-50 Stephen summarized the plight of the Jewish nation from its inception with the Abrahamic covenant through its wilderness wanderings to the establishment of the monarchy. He wasn't saying anything that his audience didn't already know and understand to be true. His tone was gentle and matter of fact. But with verse 51 he turned a corner, as is evidenced by his words "You stiff-necked people."

Throughout most of the sermon, Stephen appealed to his audience by being inclusive.

He showed that throughout their history it was "us" against "them." But with verse 51 he transferred his listeners from "us" to "them," right alongside Israel's enemies. Undoubtedly, the men of Israel didn't like his accusation. In Stephen's estimate their ancestors had resisted the Holy Spirit. Their fathers had persecuted the prophets.

They had betrayed and murdered the Righteous One. They were the recipients of the law, but they had not kept it. Stephen proclaimed what he knew to be true.

The Jews' blood boiled. In recent days there had been growing antagonism toward the early church, inflamed by the flagrant disobedience of some church leaders against the establishment. The temperature began to rise when Peter and John had disobeyed the religious leaders' order to stop preaching and teaching in the name of Jesus (see Acts 4:18), and it had continued to escalate when the men filled all Jerusalem with His teaching, as is evidenced by the flogging they received in Acts 5:40. The leaders had had enough. Stephen had cut through to the quick and accused the Sanhedrin of not keeping the law. Keeping the law was something they prided themselves on. At that point, the clouds broke, and the storm erupted.

The Jewish leaders rushed Stephen and stoned him to death. It was customary when stoning people to throw them from a high peak, then, if the fall didn't kill them, to throw rocks at them and roll boulders onto them until they died. It was a horrible way to die. Stephen didn't resist. His final prayer shows no anger toward God or toward his killers (see Acts 7:60). As Jesus had prayed from the cross,

135

Stephen demonstrated an acceptance of his fate and a concern for the souls of those who attacked him. But those who killed him weren't the last thing he saw. Before he died, Stephen saw the glory of God (see Acts 7:55).

Heidi wasn't a member of the Beverly Hills church, and she wasn't the typical person you would expect to go on a mission trip. A professional dancer, she had performed on stages around the world, including New York and Las Vegas. Before attending "the little church down the hill," as she calls it, she had attended church during only two other periods in her life. Her first experience was at a legalistic, Bible-thumping church that made her feel unwanted, unnecessary, and unclean. Several years later, she attended a church in New York with friends. There somebody stole her expensive watch, and later she caught some church people snorting cocaine at a party. She decided not to go back to that church. Nevertheless, her spiritual longing continued.

During one of the first Sundays Heidi attended the Beverly Hills church; Pastor Tom invited everyone to join the mission team. Heidi jumped at the chance. Because she was unemployed, she had to withdraw $500 from her savings account to pay the travel expenses, but she didn't give it a second thought. Her boyfriend signed up too. The trip changed her life. She says she thinks about the mission trip every day. It marks True North for her, helping her adjust her priorities. Expensive clothes and jewelry no longer impress her, and she left show business so that she can redirect her energies to help people. Every Friday evening she teaches modern dance to inner-city children at the Rampart Youth Center.

"When I grow up," one of her students said, "I want to be a teacher just like you."

As Heidi recounted the story, her eyes moistened, and her voice trembled. During the silence that followed, I heard the rustling of angels' wings. I wasn't looking into the face of a Las Vegas dancer anymore. I was looking into the face of an angel—a ministering angel. Ministry had changed Heidi. It had given her a sense of calling and purpose.

She will never be the same.

Sometimes ministry is something huge, like giving your life for the sake of the gospel. Other times it is a small thing, like giving dance lessons to an underprivileged child. Whether a ministry is large or small, it meets a need, fulfills your calling, and brings glory to God—and that is no small thing.

GLOSSARY

AUTHENTIC RELATIONSHIPS: Interactions in which people are free to take off their masks; lay down the illusion that everything is all right; and share their deepest needs and hurts in an environment of acceptance, compassion, and support.

BUSYNESS: A constant stream of endless activity.

CELEBRATION: Acknowledging God's goodness and faithfulness through your sorrow.

CELEBRATING GOD'S PRESENCE: Recognizing God's goodness and glory, even in difficult circumstances, and finding joy in His presence.

CONFESSION: Agreeing with God about your sin.

CONNECTION: Relationships of mutual accountability and support with other believers.

DEFINING MOMENT: A critical juncture when you must make a decision that will have significant ramifications for the future direction of your life.

FOCUS: A single-minded devotion to and enduring pursuit of God.

KOINONIA: Fellowship with God and with others in the body of Christ.

GLORY: Weighty importance and shining majesty that accompany God's presence.

HEARTFELT PRAYER: Prayer that arises from an intense desire to experience and be transformed by God's presence.

138

HOPE: Experiencing God's presence in any circumstance through the indwelling Christ.

INTIMACY WITH GOD: A personal love relationship with God in which we enjoy His presence and seek a deeper knowledge of His character, His will, and His ways.

LAMENT: Inviting God into your sorrow and experiencing His presence in the depths of your pain.

LECTIO DIVINA: Divine reading.

MEDITATION: An encounter with God through a concentrated focus on and application of His Word.

MINISTRY: Participating with God and cooperating with His people to fulfill His purposes.

PRAISE: Giving glory to God, regardless of your circumstances.

SABBATH REST: Remembering what life's purpose is and renewing a spirit of trust in God; a conscious choice to submit to God.

SACRIFICE: Giving up our agenda to embrace God's mission.

SERVICE: Ministering to others in Jesus' name and with His love to meet their needs, fulfill our calling, and bring glory to God.

SILENCE: Removing distractions to recalibrate your soul to God's heartbeat.

SOLITUDE: A distraction-free environment to slow down and listen to God.

SPIRITUAL DISCIPLINES: Small things Christians intentionally do to open themselves to God's work of conforming them to the image of Christ.

SPIRITUAL TRANSFORMATION: God's work of changing a believer into the likeness of Jesus by creating a new identity in Christ and by empowering a lifelong relationship of love, trust, and obedience to glorify God.

TRUE FELLOWSHIP: A relationship of unity among members of the body of Christ, characterized by sacrificial love, sharing, support, compassion, grace, sacrifice, and service.

WORSHIP: An encounter with the living God that leads us to express our love, adoration, and reverence for Him.

UNPLUGGING: A planned respite from constant connection to the world.

ENDNOTES

[1] Merrill C. Tenney, *Zondervan Pictorial Encyclopedia of the Bible* (Grand Rapids, MI: Zondervan, 1975), 179.

[2] Altapedia Online, "Republic of Liberia," http://www.atlapedia.com/online/countries/liberia.htm (accessed 3/25/2008)

[3] Charles M Sheldon, *In His Steps* (Philadelphia: Judson Press, 1933), 15.

[4] William Barclay, *The Gospel of John, Vol 1*(Philadelphia: The Westminster Press, 1955), 83.

[5] The phrase "My hour" also appears in John 7:30; 8:20; 12:23, 27; 13:1 and 17:1. Each of these instances point to his sacrificial death on the cross—his life mission.

[6] Raymond E. Brown, ed, The Anchor Bible, Vol 29: Gospel According to John I-XII, (Garden City: Doubleday, 1966), 100.

[7] Dallas Willard, *The Spirit of the Disciplines: Understanding How God Changes Lives* (San Francisco: Harper San Francisco, 1990), 9.

[8] James C. Wilhoit, *Spiritual Formation as if the Church Mattered: Growing in Christ through Community* (Grand Rapids: Baker Academic, 2008), 93.

[9] John Wooden, *Wooden on Leadership* (New York: McGraw-Hill, 2005), 135.

[10] "Bullfighter wiped out by mosquito", http://sify.com/news/fullstory.php?id=14527487 (accessed 3/28/2008)

[11] "For want of a Nail Rhyme" http://www.rhymes.org.uk/for_want_of_a_nail.htm (accessed 3/28/2008)

[12] Graham Tibbetts, "Key that could have saved the Titanic " http://www.telegraph.co.uk/news/main.jhtml?xml=/news/2007/08/29/ntitanic129.xml (accessed 3/28/2008)

[13] Jore Valencia, "Making Mom Proud," *Dodgers Magazine*, Volume 14, Number 2, 2001, 33.

[14] Roy Edgemon and Barry Sneed, *Jesus by Heart* (Nashville: LifeWay, 1999), 10.

[15] Gary L Thomas, *Seeking the Face of God: The Path to a More Intimate Relationship with Him* (Eugene: Harvest House Publishers, 1999), 78.

[16] Oz Guinness, *The Call, Finding and Fulfilling The Central Purpose of Your Life* (Nashville: Word Publishing, 1998), 106.

[17] Barbara Brown Taylor, "Divine Subtraction," *The Christian Century*, 11/3/99, 3.

[18] Edwin Markham, "Outwitted" http://holyjoe.net/poetry/markham.htm, (accessed 9/24/2008)

[19] Warren G. Bennis and Robert J. Thomas, *Geeks and Geezers: How Era, Values and Defining Moments*

Shape Leaders (Boston: Harvard Business School Press, 2002), 19.

[20] Robnoxious, "Man's Body Lies Undisturbed for 20 Years" http://www.goofball.com/news/200406111001 (accessed, 3/28/2008)

[21] Craig Barnes, *When God Interrupts: Finding New Life Through Unwanted Change* (Downers Grove, IL" InterVarsity Press, 1996), 36-37.

[22] M. Robert Mulholland Jr., *Invitation to a Journey: A Road Map for Spiritual Formation* (Downers Grove, IL:InterVarsity Press, 1993), 108.

[23] Harry Chapin, "Cat's in the Cradle" [online, cited 24 September 2008]. Available from the Internet: *www.lyricsdepot.com/hariy-cbapin/cats-in-the-cradle.*

[24] Andy Stanley, *Choosing to Cheat: Who Wins When Family and World Collide* (Portland, OR: Multnomah, 2003), 32.

[25] Audrey Barrick, "Survey: Christians Too Busy for God," *Christian Today* [online], 31 July 2007 [cited 2 May 2008]. Available from the Internet: *www.cbristiantoday.com/article/survey.christians.too.busy. for.god/ii977.htm.*

[26] Ibid.

[27] Bruce Demarest, *Satisfy Your Soul Restoring the Heart of Christian Spirituality* (Colorado Springs: NavPress Publishing Group, 1999), 94.

28 Henry Blackaby and Richard Blackaby, *Experiencing God Day by Day: A Devotional and Journal* (Nashville: Broadman & Holman, 1997), 125.

29 Tenney, Zondervan Pictorial Encyclopedia of the Bible, 5:245.

30 Malcolm Gladwell, *The Tipping Point: How Little Things Can Make a Big Difference* (Boston: Back Bay Books, 2002), 165.

31 Gary L. Thomas, *Sacred Pathways: Discover Your Soul's Path to God* (Grand Rapids, MI: Zondervan, 2002), 165.

32 Bruce Demarest, *Soul Guide: Following Jesus as Spiritual Director* (Colorado Springs: NavPress Publishing Group, 2003), *95.*

33 Mulholland, *Invitation to a Journey,* 27.

34 Thomas, *Seeking the Face of God*, 104—5.

35 "Power Plant Shut to Tune Piano," Planet Ark World Environment News [online, cited 2 June 2008]. Available from the Internet: www.planetark.org/dailynewsstory.cfin/newsid/253r4/newsDate/3IMay-2oo4/ story.

36 Mulholland, *Invitation to a Journey,* 28.

37 Henri J. M. Nouwen, *The Way of the Heart: Connecting with God Through Prayer, Wisdom, and Silence* (San Francisco: Harper San Francisco, 1981), 65.

38 Thomas, *Seeking the Face of God*, 107.

39 "Zoe Baby Name" [cited 5 June 2008]. Available from the Internet: *www.habyzone.com/babynames/babynamedisplay.asp?ID-29311*

40 "October 27, 1997 mini-crash" [online], 15 October 2008 [cited 4 September 2008]. Available from the Internet: *http//en.wikipedia.org/wiki/October 27,_ 1997_ mini-crash.*

41 Michael Card, *A Sacred Sorrow* (Colorado Springs: NavPress, 2005), 127.

42 Demarest, *Satisify Your Soul*, 171.

43 Elizabeth Achtemeier, "Preaching the Praises and Laments," *Calvin Theological Journal 36* no. *1* (2001): 105.

44 Richard Beck, "The Winter Experience of Faith: Empirical, Theological, and Theoretical Perspectives," *Journal of Psychology and Christianity* 26, no1 (2007): 76.

45 Brad Waggoner, *The Shape of Faith to Come: Spiritual Formation and the Future of Discipleship* (Nashville: B&H Publishers, 2008), 236.

46 Ibid., 242.

47 Mulholland, *Invitation to a Journey*, 146.

48 Kristine Suna-Koro, "The Ecstasy of Lament: Opera as a Model of Theology," *Theology Today* 63, no. 1 (2006): 68.

49 Samuel Alito, "Samuel Auto nomination remarks:

He notes 'the limited role that the courts play in our constitutional system,' *MSNBC* [online, cited 01 July 2008]. Available from the Internet: *www.msnbc.msn.com/id/9875730.*

[50] John Newton, 'Amazing Grace! How Sweet the Sound!" *Baptist Hymnal* (Nashville: LifeWay Worship, 2008), 104.

[51] Jim L. Wilson, "Cast your Vote: Is a 'Revolution' coming to the American Church?" Advance [online, cited 30 June 2008]. Available from the Internet: *www.pursuantgroup.com/leadnet/advancemaro6s2survey.*

[52] George Barna, *Revolution: Finding Vibrant Faith Beyond the Walls of the Sanctuary* (Ventura: Barnabooks, 2005), 115—16.

[53] Glenn McDonald, *The Disciple—Making Church: From Dry Bones to Spiritual Vitality* (Grand Haven, MI, FaithWalk Publishing, 2007), 98.

[54] This definition is a compilation of the 16 New Testament verses in which the KJV translates *ministry* from the Greek word *diakonia.*

[55] Gerhard Kittel, *Theological Dictionary of the New Testament* (Grand Rapids: Wm. B. Eerdmans Publishing Company, 1964), 2:87.

[56] "Dara" is a pseudonym. Name withheld for security reasons. "Ministry in the Midst of Conflict," doctor of ministry postseminar paper, Golden Gate Baptist Theological Seminary, 2007.

[57] Katherine Albers, "Karen Watson's duffel bag a symbol of sacrifice, students told," *Baptist Press* [online], April 2004 [cited 3July 2008]. Available from the Internet: *www.bpnews.net/bpnews.asp?id18019.*

[58] Erin Curry," 'Keep sending missionaries,' Karen Watson wrote in letter" [online], 24 March 2004 [cited 3July 2008). Available from the Internet: *wwwbpnewsnet/bpnews.asp?id=17918.*

[59] "Ministry in the Midst of Conflict."

[60] Trent C. Butler, *Holman Illustrated Bible Dictionary* (Nashville: Holman, 2003), *655.*